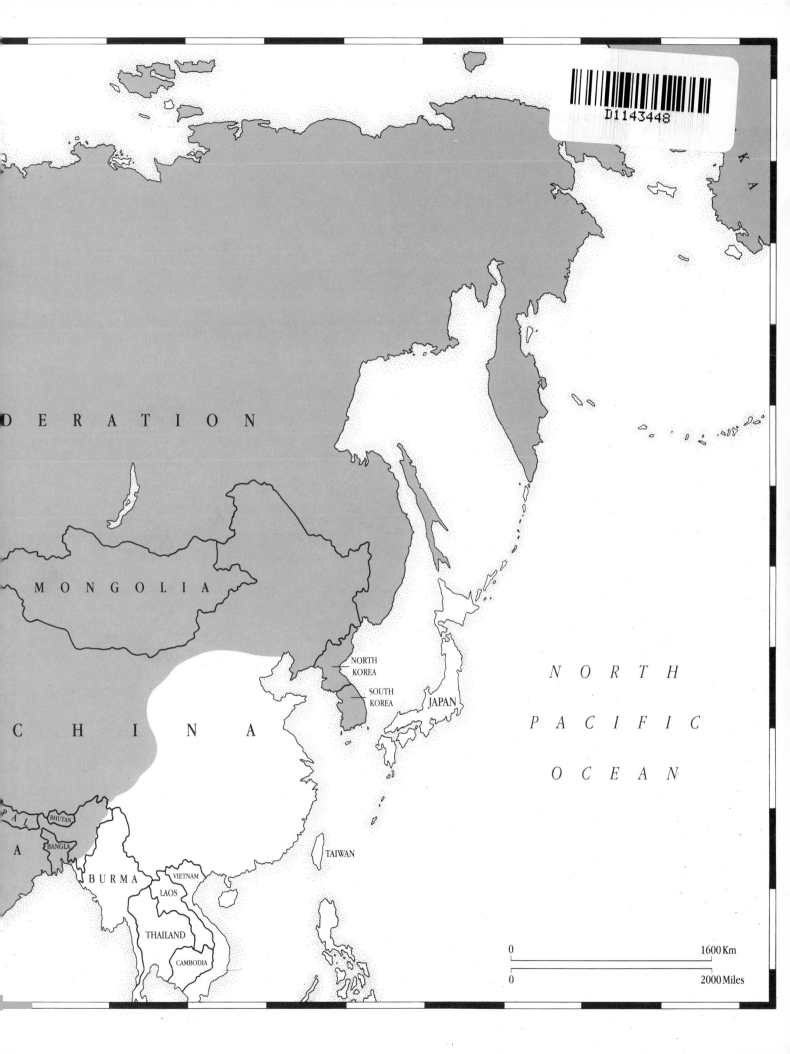

DERATION

MONGOLIA

CHINA

NORTH
KOREA

SOUTH
KOREA

JAPAN

NORTH

PACIFIC

OCEAN

NEPAL

BHUTAN

BANGLA

BURMA

VIETNAM

LAOS

THAILAND

CAMBODIA

TAIWAN

| 0 | 1600 Km |
| 0 | 2000 Miles |

—THE—
COMPLETE
WOLF

THE
COMPLETE
WOLF

LIZ BOMFORD

B☘XTREE
in association with
Tigress Productions
and Meridian Broadcasting

ACKNOWLEDGEMENTS

The study of wolves in the field is a slow and laborious task and I owe a great debt of gratitude to the biologists upon whose work I have relied in preparing this book. Many have devoted their lives to the study of wolves and my obligation to them is especially profound, not only for their scientific observations but also for the effort they have made to communicate in accessible prose.

I am particularly grateful for the information and material assistance that I have received from Dr. L. David Mech, Professor Dimitry Bibikov and Dr. David Macdonald. A number of other individuals and organizations have made important contributions: Jeremy Bradshaw of Tigress Productions (London), Grupo Lobo (Portugal); the International Wolf Center (United States); Association pour la Protection des Animaux Sauvages (France); Professor J. C. Blanco of ICONA (Spain); Richard and Julia Kemp (England), Dr. Luigi Boitani (Italy), Dr. George Schaller (Wildlife Conservation Society). Betty Veal helped research folklore; Graham Hatherley assisted with research on the paleontology and Dr. Peter Overstall gave endless encouragement and invaluable assistance with the final manuscript. Finally, I would like to thank my editor at Boxtree, Susanna Wadeson, for her kind support.

First published in Great Britain in 1993 by Boxtree Limited

Text © Liz Bomford 1993

Designed by Sarah Hall
Typeset by SX Composing Ltd, Rayleigh, Essex
Printed and bound in Italy for

Boxtree Limited
Broadwall House
21 Broadwall
London SE1 9PL

A CIP catalogue entry for this book is available from the British Library.

ISBN 1 85283 422 6

CONTENTS

CHAPTER ONE

THE WOLF OF FROST AND FIRE

That day the children were very excited. A wolf was coming to visit the school. Before it arrived, their teacher asked them to paint a picture of a wolf. They all drew fierce animals with big fangs. Later the wolf came. Afterwards their teacher asked them to draw another picture. This time there were no fangs. All the pictures showed wolves with very big feet.

Wolf Education Programme. Story from Barry Holstun Lopez, *Of Wolves and Men* (Scribners, 1978)

Wolves exert a powerful influence on our imagination, even in countries where they have been absent for hundreds of years. Like us in the West, the Chinese have their version of "Little Red Riding Hood" and share the same strong feelings of fascination and fear. We all know something about wolves – so we believe – learned from parents and grandparents, from storybooks and latterly from wildlife films and books. Perhaps no other animal has been so thoroughly studied and so well documented, yet certainly no other animal has been so grossly misrepresented. Even in this century the wolf retains its mystery, as elusive today as at any time in its past.

Wolf and man evolved together out of the last Ice Age. On every continent animals suffered from the rapid shifts in climate that occurred during that period – nearly three-quarters of all species died in North America 12,000 years ago – but wolf and man were both adaptable and found a habitat in which they could thrive in the frigid lands of the Holarctic.

This is the wolf's natural territory, an area that stretches around most of the northern hemisphere above latitude 30 degrees north. In some parts of this range, such as in Canada and the Russian Federation, wolves are ubiquitous, occupying farmland as well as wilderness. Although the wolf is not a rare animal in these regions, many local wolf populations elsewhere are now endangered, for they have been savagely persecuted.

At this critical point in time, it is more important than ever to avoid fantasy so that we may unravel the real natural history of the wolf. Can we retrace our cultural footsteps to discover the truth about our strange love–hate relationship with this predator? Today, hardly anyone sees wild wolves beyond the confines of a zoo or a park. Even in countries where wolves are numerous, they have become extremely shy. Hundreds of thousands of hours have been spent studying the species, but only a tiny fraction of that effort has been spent watching wolves unobserved. Whatever is said about the wolf, the opposite is often true. It is a voracious killer, yet it shares its food and is a gentle, playful parent. It is a "cowardly thief," yet a brave and skillful hunter. The tenderness of wolves can be deeply moving: like humans, wolves care for each other, yet they often kill their own kind.

Perhaps only those people who still lead lives very close to nature, such as the Nunamiut, the inland Eskimos of Alaska's high Arctic, know enough about the environment to understand the wolf. The inland mountain ranges of Alaska are one of the harshest environments in the world. No agriculture is possible here, and until the introduction of guns, wolves and Nunamiut hunters coexisted on an equal footing. Even today both are dependent for survival on an intimate knowledge of the environment. For native American people, the wolf is not a competitor but a teacher. They respect it as a fellow-hunter and watch its movements closely, for the activities of wolves reflect the movements of prey. Biologist Robert Stephenson drew on the Nunamiut hunters' acute powers of observation while gathering data on wolves living in the Brooks Range in 1972. He found that they viewed the wolf "as an animal whose behaviour changes perceptibly with age and experience because, like people, it learns throughout its life." An old Nunamiut hunter was asked who knew more about the mountains and the foothills, about hunting and surviving in the Brooks Range, an old man or an old wolf? After a pause he replied, "The same. They know the same."

The rest of the world has reinvented the wolf out of ignorance to satisfy a wide range of human needs. Wolf issues are a minefield of prejudice, politics, hatred, sentimentality and folklore. Underpinning all that, the wolf has been a spiritual emblem, confusingly representing both good and evil for thousands of years. These inconsistent attitudes are deeply embedded in our consciousness. The wolf is our best friend. The first animal ever to be domesticated, it was a wolf cub that lay by our fireside 13,000 years ago. Selective breeding turned it into the dogs we know today. We chose the wolf as our companion not only for its vigilance and hunting skills, but also for its caring and playful temperament. Excavations have uncovered the bones of cuddly lap-dogs that were bred long before domestic breeds of cattle.

A clever brain and manipulative hands have equipped mankind to make a living in many different ways. When we run out of space in our biological niche, we make a new one. We continually alter the environment to suit ourselves. Our talents are enormous. We can communicate knowledge right around the planet to anyone who cares to listen. We have access to thousands of years of cumulative experience laid down for posterity in the form of books. We can specialize in occupations that have no connection with food gathering, yet we still eat. Although we think of ourselves as highly developed, the reason the human population seethes across the surface of the earth is that we are crafty generalists.

Wolves by comparison are specialist carnivores. Large wild dogs, their bodies are as lean as shadows, equipped with long rangy legs and large stubby toes to aid running. Numerous local names describe the wolf in its various habitats around the world. There are Arctic wolves, timber wolves, Steppe wolves, Asian wolves and desert wolves, to name but a few. They are all members of a single species; the Gray wolf (*Canis lupus*). Minor differences in skull size and coat color distinguish one from another, but there are substantial differences in size

Previous page: Patricia Tucker takes a tame wolf called Kuani *on tours around schools as part of an education scheme to allay needless fear of wolves.*

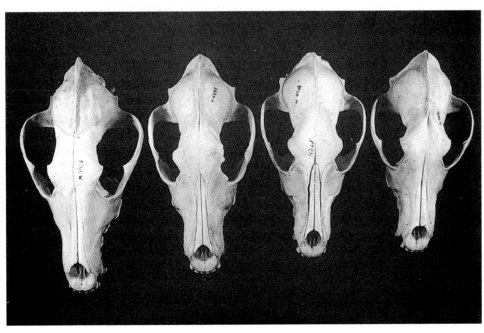

Left: Desert wolf (female).
Right: Asian wolf (female).
Below: Male skulls.
Different habitats have created several races of gray wolf. The smallest wolf in the world, the Desert wolf, Canis lupus arabs, *is adapted to survive in arid areas of the Middle East. Its larger neighbor, the Asian wolf,* Canis lupus pallipes, *has a more widespread distribution. Studies of Israeli wolf skulls show that wolves decrease in size from north to south.*

Severe conditions are no threat to the Gray wolf which evolved into the species we know today as a result of the harsh and changeable climate of the Holarctic during the last Ice Age.

between the Gray wolves found in warm climates and those of colder lands. The wolves of Israel, India and Arabia, are small, weighing as little as 26 pounds (11.79 kg) and standing only 25 inches (63.5 cm) at the shoulder. However, the wolves of northern lands have a powerful physique. They measure up to 6 feet (182.88 cm) long, nose to tail, and stand around 30 inches (76.20 cm) at the shoulder. Most wolves from North America and Russia weigh between 80 and 120 pounds (36.28–54.42 kg), but a few individuals weigh much more. The heaviest Alaskan wolf on record weighed 175 pounds (79.38 kg).

Wolves are knit together with enviable stamina and tremendous hardiness. They are particularly well adapted to survive extremes of cold. When the temperature drops to −20 degrees Celsius, human breath freezes to icicles on parka hoods. The icy chill claws at our bones. We stay indoors. The wolf, however, lopes on, for severe conditions make prey especially vulnerable and the wolf's ancestors did not survive the last glacial period of the Ice Age by missing opportunities. At −30 degrees, perhaps the wolf will curl up in some hollow, or even out in the open, where the wind soon blows the snow around its body. Snow is the best blanket of all, and insulated within a fur coat of almost unparalleled density and warmth, the wolf seems indestructible.

The environment is the motor behind the evolution of wolves, as it is for all other forms of life on earth. In its gentler aspects it is like a multidimensional kaleidoscope of subtle pressures and influences, but ultimately it is death which shapes the physical form and mental aptitudes of the living. The quality and timing of that death are crucial. All must die, but those who live long enough to

Coyotes are sometimes mistaken for wolves, for the two species are very closely related and can interbreed. Lighter in build, the coyote's jaws are less powerful and the face appears rather fox-like.

breed bestow their genes on the next generation. Within the wolf-pack only the strongest, the cleverest and most courageous get to be ancestors.

"What big teeth you've got, Grandma!" Certain wolfish characteristics are unmistakable and if we are to discover just what it is to be "wolf" we must sift through the bony debris of time, picking at clues. The story is convoluted by the wolf's tendency to disperse over vast distances in search of new hunting grounds, and by its ability to hybridize. Moreover, paleontologists must work with data which may be grossly unrepresentative. A dangerous bog may trap animals over thousands of years and ultimately yield huge quantities of fossil skeletons – but does this natural graveyard represent a cross section of the entire fauna? Probably not, but that's all there is. Fortunately paleontologists can read a tooth like a book. This is just as well, for half a jawbone may have to underpin several million years of conjecture. Absolute proof is rare and so what follows must be regarded as the scenic route through prehistory.

Fifty million years ago (just as the very first primates were developing) the planet cooled, causing the tropical forests that dominated the earth to shrink back. New combinations of vegetation began to thrive in the open spaces as vast plains, steppes and prairies unrolled. Evicted from the disappearing forest, a few carnivores began to take advantage of the new landscape. Known as miacids, they began to swap arborial traits for characteristics more suited to a ground-dwelling existence. Meanwhile, their erstwhile neighbors sharpened up their evolutionary act among the trees. Retaining their useful retractile claws, they perfected a method of hunting based on stealth, ambush and death-by-stabbing to become saber-toothed tigers and leopards. By Miocene times (24 million years ago) the crucial differences between cat and dog, formed by the exigencies of forest and plain, had become established.

High in the branches, under pressure from avian predators as well as dogs and cats, the first prosimians – our own ancestors – were laying down the primate lineage. They developed good frontal vision, useful for catching insects and essential for judging distances. Strong jumping legs allowed them to climb and leap from branch to branch without falling, while social organization and a range of meaningful cries allowed warning of danger to be broadcast. The changing landscape accelerated their evolution too. By the Miocene period they showed sufficient promise to be termed hominids.

With the land long cleared of dinosaurs, the blossoming plains served as nurseries for a proliferation of ungulates such as early forms of horses, camels, rhinoceroses and bovids. As the prairie flora diversified, vast numbers of grazing animals, each with its own particular bite to define its niche, spread across the land. In turn, a cast of predators evolved to prey upon them.

The first animal we can call "wolfish" emerged in North America. Johnston's dog (*Canis lepophagus*) was more of a scavenger than a hunter, a small canid following in the bloodsoaked trail of the great amphicyonid "bear dogs" which held the position of top predator until 5.5 million years ago. Versatile and opportunistic, Johnston's dog was a lean creature, capable of covering very long distances in its search for carrion and small prey. It soon spread across the Beringian land-bridge to colonize Eurasia, where it became known as the Arno dog, giving rise in the Old World to the ancestors of the smaller jackals. Back on the American continent the New World descendants of Johnston's dog are coyotes.

It was the savage, changeable climate of the Holarctic that fashioned the first true wolf. The joining of Old and New Worlds by the Beringian connection created a vast landmass and here, out of Johnston's and Arno dog stock, a larger-proportioned canid evolved. The new Etruscan wolf (*Canis etruscans*) had a broader, more powerful muzzle enabling it to overcome large prey on its own account. Its teeth were adapted to seize flesh, to slice meat and to crack bone. Armed with the tools of a specialist carnivore, the Etruscan wolf was a woodland dweller and almost certainly a social animal, like its descendant *Canis lupus*, the wolf we know today.

Other wolves sprang up in a wave of speciation. Traces of Armbruster's wolf or Falconer's wolf in Eurasia and North America show a tendency towards broader muzzles, and a more carnivorous dentition was firmly established. This wolfish trend endowed the top dogs with the power to dominate ever-larger prey, but their progenitors, the little dogs, continued to thrive and may even have shared the same hunting grounds, occupying a different niche.

Our own Gray wolf (*Canis lupus*) arose in Eurasia sometime during the early Pleistocene period, evolving to exploit the challenging new conditions thrown up by the last Ice Age. Although scientists usually refer to the Pleistocene (from 1.8 million years ago up to around 10,000 years ago) as the Ice Age, this is a misleading label. The Earth has in fact experienced many Ice Ages and the last cold snap was relatively insignificant with one enormous exception. What happened during this period of time laid the foundations of man's prehistory. Those climatic events created the environment we live in today.

It was not a period of continuous glaciation and bitter cold but characterized by oscillating climatic conditions – for a while, parts of North America even enjoyed a subtropical climate. Over most of the Holarctic innumerable shifts of global temperature caused ice sheets to come and go, breaking up the surface of the earth under the pressures generated by freezing and thawing, encouraging the development of a rich colonizing flora on the crumbly soils left behind.

The Pleistocene was paradise for the newly minted Gray wolf. Horses filled the plains together with countless caribou, camels and buffalo. Burgeoning herds of ungulates moved between the summer pastures at the edge of the ice and winter shelter among the trees of the taiga. Exposed by falling sea-levels, the lush meadows of the Beringia land-bridge enticed the caribou and musk-oxen to populate a new continent. The horses that had arisen in North America migrated to Eurasia. With so many animals on the move, the wolves only needed to follow in order to feed on those who died of natural causes, the old and the newborn. As wolf numbers rose, they adapted their behavior to hunt in a pack in order to kill rather than simply scavenge. Conditions suited wolves so well that they became the most widely distributed mammal in the world. They dominated not only the richest environments but the marginal lands of mountain and desert as well, where the smaller subspecies evolved to suit quite different conditions. In response to what must have been heavy predation, the ungulates developed longer legs and a physique adapted for running extremely fast. The legbones of the horse fused together for strength, enabling it to gallop on the tip of its middle finger, the nail we call a hoof.

The Gray wolf could never run quite as fast, although its bones also fused and its legs grew long with trying, but it could run for longer. Incredible stamina powered this predator across two continents in the voyage towards its modern form. From Eurasia it made its way back to North America around 750,000 years ago.

It had the legs and stamina to run down its prey, the strength and the teeth to grasp it and throw it to the ground. It had the social skills to breed and hunt as a pack – but in North America the Gray wolf was not the top dog. An extraordinary beast, the Dire wolf, had arisen from Falconer's wolf descent to hunt the giant herbivores that were sweeping over the prairies. The Dire wolf was massively constructed, at least 20 percent heavier than the largest wolf we know today. Its strong shoulders, deep chest and heavy pelvis spoke of a new purpose. With shorter feet and tremendously powerful legs, a pack of Dire wolves could bring down a mammoth, a mastodon or a Giant sloth, and when these were not available they would scavenge the kills of mega-predators such as the Saber-toothed tiger. For half a million years, up until 7,500 years ago, the Dire wolf was the commonest type in North America.

The Gray wolf slipped unobtrusively into the landscape, preying on medium-sized herbivores such as deer, and clearing up after the kills of larger predators. The two wolves coexisted for nearly 400,000 years, although the Dire wolf was always dominant. Excavations show they travelled in packs up to fifty or sixty strong, and that the Dire wolf occupied a much larger portion of the New World than the Gray wolf which never ventured into South America. It occupied the mountainous areas of the north, terrain in which the heavier Dire wolf was at a disadvantage.

Then fate, in the form of climatic change, altered everything. During the Wisconsin period, from 16,500 to 8,000 years ago, just as human hunters using more sophisticated weapons were beginning to have a serious effect on prey, the climate became particularly unstable. The largest herbivores could not adapt quickly enough to changing patterns of plant growth. Burdened with extended life cycles and slow rates of reproduction, they became vulnerable and the mammoth, mastodon and Giant sloth died out. A wave of extinctions swept around the Earth. Even the horse was lost from the Americas.

Deprived of the prey on which it depended, the Dire wolf slipped into extinction, probably in the way that has become all too familiar to biologists studying endangered species in the twentieth century. At first it would produce fewer offspring, for most of the pups would tend to die during their first winter. Year after year the pattern would be repeated as food resources failed. Then, with no new generations coming along, the population would crash. Finally there would be only a scattering of individuals left, not enough to find partners in order to breed. It would be cheering to believe that in these desperate straits, Dire wolves behaved as endangered wolves do in modern times by cross-breeding with the insurgents. This would have mingled the last of their genes with those of the future – but we do not know if this occurred.

The Gray wolf was well equipped to take over. Its customary wide-ranging habits enabled it to repopulate the Dire wolf's North American territory almost at once. With the mega-herbivores gone, there was plenty of grazing for moose (European elk) and deer, the natural prey of a fleet-footed hunter, while musk-oxen and caribou (wild reindeer) were thriving in the far north. It must have seemed as though Gray wolves had inherited the earth! It looks as though their first act was to drive their rivals, the coyotes, out into the arid lands of the American West.

Wolves and men . . . both evolved in the unstable conditions of the Ice Age. The cold was no problem. Although the icy fingers of glaciers extended as far south as Nevada in North America and the Severn estuary in England, they were not only instruments of destruction but also agents of rapid change that directly benefitted wildlife. The grinding action of the ice scoured the rocks to create mud and finally fertile soil. As the shifting ice withdrew, it left behind tundra, an area of subsoil permafrost which thawed into boggy ground and icy ponds in summer. No trees interrupted the emptiness, for only willow and birch shrubs and small-leaved evergreen plants such as bilberry, crowberry and dwarf rhododendron could grow. In the north, long hours of summer daylight made the plants superproductive and provided grazing for vast herds of ungulates. No, the cold was not a hardship. It was when the climate became warmer that difficulties arose, for that led to the rapid growth of forest trees which reduced the grazing habitat available. Then everyone went hungry.

In spite of the uncertainty of those times, wolves and men lived in some sort of harmony, sharing the spoils of nature according to their strength and numbers, but that relationship changed as soon as man started to manage the environment.

His first tool was fire, which he used to burn down the trees in order to create meadows for the wild ungulates on which he depended. This was the first stage in domestication, and as the hunter began to feel that he owned the prey, his mentality changed to that of a farmer. No longer an honoured teacher, the wolf became his adversary.

American elk (wapiti) are an important item of prey for wolves in North America.

Men and wolves have been locked into an extraordinarily bitter conflict ever since, a battle that has sometimes taken on the quality of a crusade in which wolves have been poisoned, hunted, captured and even tortured in the name of agriculture. Driven from much of their range in Europe, the United States and Mexico, wolves have nevertheless survived man's attempts at extermination.

For 2,000 years we have treated them as vermin. We have committed them – as Theodore Roosevelt put it so neatly – to be "the beast of waste and desolation." It was not always so. Pity the once-mighty wolf and its modern inheritance.

CHAPTER TWO

MYTH AND MAGIC

O was it wolf into the wood,
Or was it fish intill the sea,
Or was it man, or wile woman,
My true love, that misshapit thee?

"Kemp Owyne"
(traditional British ballad)

Wolves have been associated with magic and mystery from earliest times. Cast in the role of a totem animal or icon, the wolf has played an important part in the development of religious ideas in human societies on both the Eurasian and North American continents.

European mythology is made complex by centuries of faith and superstition overlaid like veneers on a framework of social order that has often changed abruptly as tribe has overrun tribe and customs have been lost or reinterpreted. While modern religion tends to be based on intellectual ideas, older beliefs sprang directly from the struggle to survive. In its passage through life the human soul has been intimately bound up with nature and the apparently magical cycles of creation.

Metaphor is one of man's most important intellectual tools, not in the sense of "figure of speech" but in the root sense of the word, meaning to "carry across" ideas, to use an image to suggest an abstract concept. The rich tapestry of mythology is profoundly animist because in early times the whole of nature served to provide images for the human imagination. Thus to understand our irrational hatred of the wolf we must understand our mythological inheritance.

The eternal philosophical questions, "Who am I and what am I doing here?" were as pertinent to Stone Age man as they are to us today. Perhaps more so, for the possibility of comprehending the mysterious workings of the environment offered an escape from its vicissitudes.

We have cheapened magic, turned it into sleight of hand, but in former times natural transformations lay behind man's deepest spiritual insights. The metamorphosis of a chrysalis into a butterfly . . . the growth of a seed into a plant . . . the turning of winter into spring . . . all these natural events were endowed with a special mystery. Transformations like these were understood to be part of a sacred process closely linked to fertility. In contrast, unnatural change was seen

A shaman painted on the walls of a cave in southern France during the last Ice Age, the Sorcerer of Trois Freres is depicted half-man, half-beast. Wolves (and other animals) played an important part in the early religious practice of Eurasia, which arose out of ceremonies associated with hunting and fertility.

Previous page: A powerful, intelligent predator, the wolf evokes great fear and hatred in humans. Curiously, its descendent the dog is man's best friend.

as magical and dangerous.

Although there are no written records, we know that this is our common culture because, wherever we come from, we share the same beliefs in magic and transformation. We have all been taught the basics at that point in our lives when we were best able to understand them, in childhood. Magic is inexplicable change. Magic is uncertainty. Magic – without the remotest possibility of trickery – is truly frightening because it unleashes the chaotic powers of the unknown.

The idea of human transformation into animal form is an extremely ancient one. The first traces of this magic are found among the cave paintings of south-western France. In the foothills of the Pyrenees, the Chapel of the Lioness in the cave of Trois Frères was clearly a place for ritual. Here stands a stalagmite carved in the form of a cave lion, battered as though it may have been struck repeatedly with weapons in the course of some dramatic reenactment. Other caves are decorated with paintings of massive aurochs (early wild cattle, relatives of the bison) and splendid prancing horses, but the most extraordinary feature of the cave of Trois Frères is set in a separate chamber, reached along a narrow ledge. Dominating the wall like a crucifix in a chapel, the image of a sorcerer dances in the flickering light. Above his pricked-up ears and shaggy, wolf-like neck, he bears antlers. His swinging genitalia, legs and feet look human, but owlish eyes stare out of a furry face. Half-man, half-beast, he is caught as though in a trance, as though in the very process of transformation.

It was a common belief in hunting societies that animals, like man, possessed a soul. Hunting was a dangerous business because the act of killing could kindle the wrath of the spirit world. It was therefore essential to negotiate a pact with the prey – or other powerful spirits – before the hunt. In this, Paleolithic Europeans seem to have shared a worldview similar to that of North American Indians.

Hunting with Stone Age weapons required courage. The hard-kicking hooves of horses, elk (moose) and wild reindeer could break bones or worse, while a butt from the horny brow of an auroch would doubtless prove fatal. Even today, razor-sharp tusks make the wild boar notoriously dangerous. In order to summon the inner strength required for hunting, exclusive brotherhoods of hunters evolved. They armed themselves with supernatural protection. Almost certainly in a trance-like state, they took on the fearless nature of wolves or bears through a process of identification with these animals. Cloaks made of animal skins were essential props in these ceremonies, and the idea of a sacred or magical cloak that could transform the wearer has persisted in European folk legend to the present day.

Disguise was also a crucial part of the initiation ceremony of the Olala from the Niska tribe in British Colombia. In a nineteenth-century description the novice "died" in a ceremony in which he appeared to have been killed. He was returned to his tribe a year later, accompanied by an artificial totem animal. From that time onward, a special relationship was seen to exist between the initiate and his totem. In *The Golden Bough* Sir James Fraser writes of "the possibility of establishing a sympathetic relation with an animal, a spirit, or other mighty being, with whom a man deposits for safe-keeping his soul or some part of it, and from whom he receives in return a gift of magical powers."

In this relationship the wolf was the mystic teacher and guide, but the idea of the soul leaving the body in a magical journey would have been understood anywhere in the Paleolithic world. The transformation demonstrates the ability of the soul to defeat death, to enter the spirit world and to return.

Wolves have been associated with death since earliest times. Among certain tribes it was the practice to expose the bodies of the dead to scavenging animals such as ravens, vultures or wolves, in order to strip away the flesh so that the bones could be buried inside the family dwelling. We know that wolf-like priests called *hirpi* served Soranus, the Sabine god of the dead. It is possible that they acted as grisly undertakers, dressed in wolf-skins, their job being to prepare bodies for storage. Anubis was the jackal-headed god of death of the pre-dynastic Egyptians (before 3000 B.C.), and in Greek mythology, Charon, the ferryman who carried the Shades across the Styx, wore wolf's ears.

Paleolithic hunting magic evolved into the worship of moon goddesses. Capricious deities such as the Greco-Roman Artemis or Diana had power not only to change their own shape, but to use magic to entrance others. The earliest known spell is described in the Akkadian *Epic of Gilgamesh* in which the goddess Ishtar turned her victim (a faithful shepherd who had made an inappropriate sacrifice to her) into a wolf, with the result that his own dogs fell upon him and ate him up. Like all parables, this memorable story works at different levels of understanding. Artemis was goddess of the hunt but she was also mistress of Earth, Air and the Underworld. In her darkest manifestation she was Hecate, goddess of Death, portrayed as such wearing three wolf-heads.

Wolves were traditionally important "totem" animals in the
native animist cultures of North America. Hunter-gatherer
communities did not perceive the wolf as a competitor, but
honoured the animal as a respected teacher and source of
spiritual guidance. However, wolves were occasionally killed
and wolf-skins were worn as ceremonial robes by shaman who
might "become" a wolf for a short time, assuming a trance to
communicate with the spiritual teacher. Healers were expected
to intervene on behalf of their patients in the spiritual world,
as well as providing practical herbal treatment.

A wolf attends the Celtic god Cernummos, depicted on the Gundestrup cauldron, a 1st or 2nd century BC ceremonial vessel thrown as an offering into a Danish lake. The pastoril nomad Celts of northern Europe worshipped gods that were closely linked to animals, harking back to the animist worship of hunter-gatherer times.

Animals were commonly sacrificed to the gods, not as gifts but as spiritual emissaries. It was not necessary to burn the body of the victim, and as a result sacrifice became so commonplace that Greek priests were often little more than butchers cutting up meat for human consumption, for they dedicated only the animal's hide and bones to the deities. However, when ominous earthly events occurred, the priests sometimes insisted that this meant the gods were dissatisfied with the quality of the usual sacrifices, and occasionally a human messenger was needed. We know that Agamemnon sacrificed his own daughter Iphigeneia, in order to bring wind to his becalmed fleet during the battle at Aulis. The high-born child was the perfect envoy to take the King's plea to Apollo, who was not only God of the Wind, but was also closely associated with wolves. Cultivated Greeks abhorred human sacrifice, but its principles were well understood.

The mountains of Arcadia were reputed to be infested with wolves, some of which were said to be lycanthropes, or werewolves, wolves which were once human in form. The wolf – *lykos* – is central to the Greek creation myth of King Lykaon who offended Zeus (who came to supper in disguise) by offering him a dish containing human flesh. It is thought that cannibalism was practised by secret societies of wolf-brotherhoods where the ceremony of sharing human flesh (the breaking of a terrifying taboo) was used to forge fearsome bonds of relationship. In this story, the enraged Zeus turned Lykaon and his sons into wolves and then unleashed the Great Flood of Deucalion upon the land. Only Deucalion and Pyrrha, who constructed an ark, survived the destruction to found the Greek nation.

The writer Pausanus, who visited the remote and inhospitable peak of Mount Lykaion (Wolf Mountain) sometime during the second century A.D., was witness to the most important ritual of the year, the annual sacrifice to the Arcadian god, Zeus Lykaeus. Although not explicit, Pausanus implies (horror-struck) that a human sacrifice was made. The people of Arcadia believed that during this ceremony one of their number was transformed into a wolf and banished for nine years to wander the countryside living as a wild beast. If the werewolf tasted human flesh during his period of banishment he would be condemned to live out the rest of his life in animal form, otherwise he could resume his human shape. In modern times archaeologists digging through the 4½ feet (1.3 m) of ashy deposit that lay under the altar on Mount Lykaion have found no trace of human remains although the animal bones discovered there dated back to at least 600 B.C. Perhaps it was all sleight of hand by the magician priest. Certainly, whatever really happened during the ceremony, human sacrifice and transformation were believed to occur.

Book Ten of Homer's *Odyssey* is rich in wolf-clan references. In this eighth-century B.C. epic, the hero Odysseus returns from the Trojan War to be greeted by his grandfather Autolykos, whose name means "He who is himself a wolf." We learn that Autolykos comes from Mount Parnassus on the north side of the Gulf of Corinth where the Delphinians worshipped wolves because they believed their ancestors came from Lykoreia, another Wolf Mountain. Autolykos teaches Odysseus the dark secrets of hunting boar and it is during the hunt that the hero is wounded, receiving the scar that will act to identify him on his return to Ithaca.

The Athenians revered the wolf and ordered that any man who killed one had to pay for the animal to be buried with proper ceremony. When Athens became infested by a particularly bold pack, a sacrifice was made to Apollo at the site of the Lyceum, a place devoted to wolf-worship. Apollo was particularly associated with wolves because he was said to be the son of Leto, a she-wolf. Whether the god heeded the prayer is not recorded, but it was said that the acrid smell of burning drove the wolves away.

In Scandinavia, from the seventh century A.D., the mythology of Odin grew powerful as a creation myth for warlike Norsemen. Odin, their god of death, was particularly associated with wolves. Like a shaman, he had strange powers of transformation which allowed him to leave his body as though sleeping and assume the form of an animal.

The saga of the Volsungs dynasty, who seem to have been an archetypal wolf-clan, tells of Odin's descendant Sigmund who had a son, Sinfjötli. This boy was also Sigmund's nephew because he was conceived in an incestuous relationship with Sigmund's sister Signy. When Sinfjötli grew up, father and son roamed the dark forests in a journey of initiation. They discovered an isolated hut full of bewitched men, from whom they stole two magic wolf-skins. (One of the basic tools of the shaman was a cloak made of animal skin daubed with a hallucinatory unguent.) When they put them on they were transformed into werewolves and in this form the two men ravaged the countryside, killing large numbers of innocent people in a series of "heroic" deeds. When the appointed day came to resume their human form, Sigmund and Sinfjötli burned the wolf-skins so that they could not bring "bad luck" to anyone else.

Wolves are not the only dangerous magical creatures depicted in northern legend. There are stories of bulls, ravens, bears and many other animals; an indication of the all-embracing nature of Palearctic animism. The word "berserk" comes from the *Ynglinga Saga* of Snorri Sturluson (1179–1241), which is an early history of Sweden. In this tale are described warriors of Odin who "went without their mail-coats and were mad as hounds or wolves, bit their

In the time of the crusades, Christians cursed their Muslim enemies as "dogs," a term of abuse which may have had its origins in ancient animist practises. This Cynocephalus or dog-head was found in an Armenian gospel book.

shields, and were as strong as bears or bulls. They slew men, but neither fire nor iron had effect on them. This is called *berserkgangr* (going berserk)."

The harsh and uncompromising legends surrounding Odin served to spur on warrior jarls as they set about pillaging their neighbors. The unexpected shock of the sack of Lindisfarne Monastery in A.D. 793 reverberated across Europe. "Behold the church of St Cuthbert spattered with the blood of the priests of God, despoiled of all its ornaments; a place more venerable than all in Britain is given as prey to pagan peoples." (Contemporary account taken from K. R. G. Pendersonn, *The Vikings*, Windward, 1980.) Christian Britain had been at peace for 200 years and was plainly unready for such incursions, but above all it was the brutish savagery of the pagan Vikings that shocked commentators. Odin was a god who appreciated violent death. Vikings considered it a "glorious" fate which ensured entry to the halls of Valhalla where Odin himself would be waiting to greet the slain. The typical Viking bloodbath was a religious obligation to Odin. The wolf-god was particularly associated with hanging, as he was said to have hanged himself from Yggdrasill, the ash-tree of knowledge, in order to obtain magical powers. In recognition of this, Viking marauders

Slain by pagan Danish invaders in A.D. 870 because he would not abjure Christianity, King Edward's dismembered corpse was left in a wood, where it was later discovered with a wolf standing guard over the Saint's head.

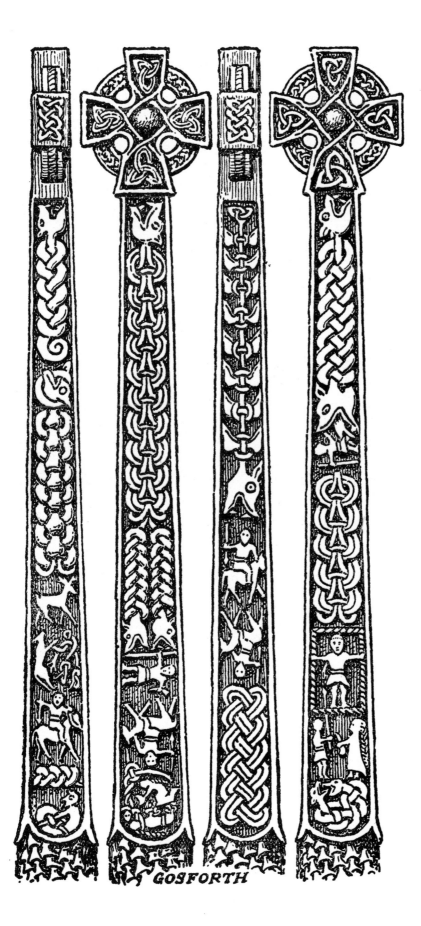

GOSFORTH

During the pre-dynastic period before about 3,000 BC., the Egyptians worshipped gods in animal form. The jackal-headed Anubis was God of Death.

Carved around A.D. 940, the fourteen foot high Viking cross that stands in the churchyard of Gosforth, England, depicts scenes from the Norse saga Voluspa. Vidar, son of Odin, is shown trying to prevent the end of the world by gagging the Fenris-wolf during the final battle of the gods.

Relief of the wolf god Tyr from Torsunda Parish Council, Oland, Sweden.

sometimes strung their victims up on feast days. Other Europeans, steeped in the sophistication of cultural developments in Southern Europe, saw the onslaught as a conflict between the pagan powers of darkness and Christianity.

The mythology of the Norse gods is complete in that it carries within itself the story of its own destruction, for it was a wolf named Fenrir that ultimately brought about the downfall of Odin and his sons in a magical battle pitched against giants and evil spirits at Ragnarok on the ethereal Vivrid Plain. A mysterious sandstone cross which still stands today in the churchyard of Gosforth in Cumberland, England, depicts Fenrir, the magical vehicle of destruction. The wolf is seen gagged by the sword of the sky god Tyr who is making a vain attempt to prevent it from freeing the powers of darkness by eating the sun and biting the moon.

The reign of fear engendered by the robber "wolves of the sea" has colored the psychological history of Western Europe. Although in Britain many Viking invaders settled down to farm and raise children, the folk memory of "berserk" men who came from the sea, penetrating the winding rivers to plunder and kill, was inextricably linked with wolves. Thus the wolf was the perfect foil for the Christian image of the Lamb of God and as such was used by the medieval Christian Church in its battle against pagan practices and witchcraft. Although medieval society appeared to be entirely devoted to the worship of God as an omnipotent divine force, what people actually believed – and, indeed, what the Church actually taught – was that two supernatural forces existed. From the metaphysical point of view, Lucifer or Satan (an angel borrowed from the Hebrew faith) was essential, for how could one teach the concept of "good" without an image of "evil"? Like the pagan Norsemen, Christians in Northern Europe had a lively sense of the world held in the grip of two opposing spiritual powers. Associated with the dark arts, with ferocity, lechery, sorcery, human sacrifice and cannibalism, the wolf was definitely on the wrong side.

In Southern Europe, the activities of fierce animist clans were comfortably integrated into modern life by the cunning of the Roman Emperor Augustus, who elevated the story of Romulus and Remus to the status of an imperial

Romulus and Remus who became the founders of Rome, were said to have been suckled by a wolf when they were abandoned as infants.

29

creation myth. The tale smacks of an earlier Cretan legend, but no matter. Romulus was reputed to have been the son of Mars by Rhea Silvia, daughter of Numitor, King of Alba Longa. Along with his twin brother Remus, he was left to die by his great-uncle Amulius who wanted to seize the throne. As the whole world knows, the twins were suckled by a wolf. They were finally found by a peasant named Faustulus and his wife Acca Larenia who raised them as their own children. Romulus is said to have founded Rome in 753 B.C. but he quarrelled with Remus whom he subsequently killed.

Faustulus and Acca Larenia probably existed and are likely to have been members of a primitive wolf-cult. Fertility rites were still a feature of these old religions, and their well-known ceremonies had led to the use of the word *lupa* for a whore in Roman society. Augustus restored the cave in which the twins were said to have been suckled, and elevated the Rites of Lupercalia, a wolf-cult fertility festival, into an important Roman celebration in honour of the founding twins. In an extraordinary move designed to raise a religion regarded as downright primitive by sophisticated Romans, the ceremony was attended by the Vestal Virgins and the most eminent members of Roman society. Suddenly the wolf-cults were respectable.

It was a shrewd strategy. *Lupus* is not a Greek or Roman word, but comes from the Sabine language. Like the Norse in later times, the Sabines were a warrior nation, retaining a good many animist practices in their wolf-centered religion. Roman armies could not defeat the ferocious Sabines in battle and so they won them over by a process of trade and cultural assimilation. Romulus and Remus became the symbols of both nations "twinned" within the concept of the City of Rome. In this spirit of tolerance, new life was breathed into the age-old image of the wolf which became the symbol of the Pax Romana and its power.

For the next 2,000 years two apparently opposing currents of belief existed in Europe. In northern lands the ferocious, demonic aspect of the wolf was emphasized, but in the south the ancient connection of wolves with fertility rites was rehabilitated. These beliefs did not entirely die out until the last century. In France, Germany and the Slavonic countries it was imagined that the wolf was a corn-spirit, the very essence of fruitfulness and bounty. When the wind passed across the fields, causing the ripening grain to ripple, the peasants would say delightedly, "The wolf is going through the corn."

At harvest, the final sheaf of corn was customarily known as the "wolf-sheaf" because as the reapers steadily circled the field, the wildlife was forced to hide in the standing corn at the centre. As the men approached the last row, rabbits and hares would flee in all directions. And sometimes a wolf. In nineteenth-century Feilenhof (East Prussia) this event was sufficiently common for the peasants to watch to see how the wolf carried its tail. Held high, it indicated the wolf's curse, poor weather for the following year and a thin harvest. Held low, it was a sign of blessing and fertility. Then the peasants would follow the wolf to offer thanks and make an offering of food, for the wolf's tail was not just a superstitious sign but was believed to have real fertilizing power. The wolf was a god, Apollo in one of his many disguises.

The spirit of the corn was at the center of a magical cycle of transformation in which man played the vital role of reaper. Cutting the corn was seen as an attack on the spirit of life, but it was one that must be made if death in autumn was to lead to rebirth in spring. The spiritual energy for this transformation was carried

The dark wolf, created by human fear is far more terrible than the living animal. However, wolves breed vigorously and there is a limit on how many large predators even the most enlightened rural communities will tolerate. In most parts of the world where wolves survive in close proximity to man, they are killed – legally or illegally – by hunters. As a result, many local populations are endangered whilst some subspecies face extinction.

Included by the Grimm Brothers in their nineteenth-century collection of
German folk stories, Red Riding Hood was actually a tale of much greater
antiquity and wilder provenance. The first written version is found in
Charles Perralt's 'Histoire ou Contes du Temps Passé' published in 1697.
The hood is a significant emblem, perhaps an indication of the magical
nature of Red Riding Hood herself. Together with wands, belts and
broomsticks; magic cloaks were a basic tool in witch craft. The predatory
wolf may have represented the occult activities of a male animist sect. In
England hoods were associated with the prehistoric worship of horses.

over from one harvest to the next by means of ceremony and fetish. The Christian Church annexed the harvest festival, but the priest could not stamp out the habit of making a sacred corn "dolly" plaited out of twisted straw. In many parts of Europe these were called "wolves" and are still made to this day.

Our mythology is the fruit of an extraordinary blossoming of the human imagination. No one can say exactly how old these ideas may be. It is, after all, only through the art of the cave paintings that we have any knowledge at all about the spiritual life of Paleolithic times. Archeology can help, but much is guesswork. We can be sure, however, that the wolf has been an important icon in the cultural pattern of both North America and Eurasia for thousands of years, for the people of both continents share a sense of the wolf as symbol of life and death, of destruction and renewal.

CHAPTER THREE

CONFRONTATION AND COHABITATION

*Each year, in March and September, they ought to go through the midst
of the forest to set traps to take the wolves in the places where they had
been found by the hounds; and if the scent was not good because of the
upturned earth, then they should go at other times in the summer (as on
St Barnabas' Day, 11 June), when the wolves had whelps, to take and
destroy them, but at no other times; and they might take with them a
sworn servant to carry the traps; they were to carry a bill-hook and
spear, and hunting knife at their belt but neither bows nor arrows; and
they were to have with them an unlawed mastiff trained to the work. All
this they were to do at their own charges, but they had no other duties to
discharge in the forest.*

The duties of the forester-of-fee, who held his land in exchange for the
responsibility of wolf-hunting. England in 1251, from Thomas Hinde,
Forests of Britain (Victor Gollancz, 1985)

Although wolves have played an important part in the development of religion,
the species was rarely protected. Even in the most forbearing societies there
seems to be a limit on how many wolves people will accept on their doorsteps.
Although wolves tend to avoid human habitation in North America today, this
was not the case when the population was high during the nineteenth century
and it is contrary to European experience. Wolves are intelligent animals which
make a living where they can, and human activities are attractive to them.

Attempts to exterminate the species in Europe started as early as the third
century B.C. when the Celts began breeding an Irish wolfhound especially for the
task. Although the aggression of wolves has been tremendously exaggerated, it
was generally true that where wolves were numerous, solitary travellers on foot
or on horseback were obliged to take special care. In the days before refrigeration
it was normal for herds of cattle to be on the road, wandering slowly towards
lucrative markets in the city, perhaps hundreds of miles distant. Not quite the
same as the massive wild migrations of yesteryear, but a magnet for predators
nevertheless.

The Anglo-Saxons dealt vigorously with the wolf problem – Alfred the Great
was a keen hunter. Wolves were so hated that the month of January was called
Wolfmonat (Wolf Month) and was set aside for their slaughter. Was the wolf
really dangerous or was this a Christian reaction to an animal associated with

35

Wolf-hunting was encouraged as a sport for English commoners, who were barred from killing the King's deer. Where wolves were numerous, wolf-hunting was obligatory for every able-bodied man on certain days each year.

Cy deuise comment on doit chasier et prendre le loup.

Previous page: For the last thousand years European wolves have been forced to live in close proximity to man as their natural prey have disappeared through overhunting.

political enemies and heathen practices? Both were probably the case. In those days people did not often pause to appreciate the aesthetic beauty of dark forests and remote countryside. Before the advent of banking, travellers were obliged to carry their wealth with them from place to place. They journeyed in fear.

In wild country "spitals" were constructed on lonely roads so that benighted travellers could rest in safety. The stonework of one such shelter can still be found just south of Glenshee in Scotland. The word "louphole" comes from "lupus hole," a chink through which the besieged could eye the foe. There were certainly many wolves in Scotland right up until the seventeenth century, but there were other beasts at large too. Like much of Europe, it was a lawless area. The rustling of cattle was so commonplace as to remain a respectable activity as late as the nineteenth century. Tribal honour was of greater significance than honesty, which made the law particularly difficult to administer. Many of the "wolves" were bipedal.

From earliest times the forests had been the traditional home of thieves and runaways from feudal bondage. The Saxons called the outlaws *wulvesheasfod* (wolf-heads) because, like wolves, they had a price on their heads. Harking back to the cult of Odin, the gallows tree was known as the "wolf-headed tree." Forget about Robin Hood! The robber "wolves" of the forest were dangerous and greatly feared, a menace down the centuries. When the Black Prince visited

Chester (a particularly unruly area) the citizens petitioned him to cut down the nearby Forest of Wirral to relieve them of the marauders.

Wolf could be turned against wolf. When a human fugitive was captured he might evade punishment (probably death) by providing a certain number of wolf-tongues. In A.D. 985, King Edgar imposed a levy of 300 wolf-skins a year on King Idwal of Wales in lieu of tribute; a demand calculated to keep hot-tempered princes out of mischief, while at the same time destroying a breeding stronghold in the remote fastnesses of the Welsh mountains. Wales ran out of wolves just three years later.

The forests of Europe were wild but they were far from being wastelands in medieval times. Wood was the primary material used for building houses, making furniture and implements and constructing ships, so plantations of trees were carefully managed by coppicing and the forests were considered to be a valuable asset. Naturally, most of them belonged to the king. Kingship was inextricably tied up with hunting, as it must have been since hunter–gatherer times. In Britain, deer and wild boar were noble beasts reserved for the royal table: the meat from both was called venison. Other animals – badgers, foxes, otters and wolves – were not protected. Quite the reverse: when it came to wolves, kings throughout Europe were only too pleased to encourage their slaughter in the belief that this would increase the population of deer.

Then as now, huntsmen worried incessantly about the population levels of game animals. Sometimes things got so bad that hunt servants had to "cart" animals from one forest to another. Thousands of miles of chestnut fencing were erected around the deer parks where game were kept in captivity. The Romans, and subsequently the Normans, brought the fallow deer (*Cervus dama*) all the way from Sicily to boost stocks, but this did not solve the problem. The King's verderers blamed poachers and wolves for the disappearance of red deer, Britain's most prized game animal, although in hindsight this was probably caused by deforestation and hundreds of years of overhunting.

A tapestry after Johannes Bol, woven in 1589, shows a contemporary wolf-hunt with the comment, "Thus the wolf is captured, either tempted by a bait of blood, or in a net, or with a stout pike."

In the thirteenth century the English King Edward I decided to exterminate the wolf once and for all. In 1281 he employed Peter Corbet "to take and destroy all the wolves he can find in . . . Gloucestershire, Worcestershire, Herefordshire, Shropshire and Staffordshire." Corbet was almost completely successful. Wolves are said to have consumed the deer in a park at Fawley in 1290, but that was the end of it. The wolf was gone from England. An iron wolf's head was

The population of wolves in Europe has ebbed and flowed in response to the activities of man. Wolves traditionally thrive during periods of warfare.

placed on the door of the church at Abbey Dore, Herefordshire, in celebration.

The loss of the wolf certainly did not halt the decline of deer stocks, however. Although once very common, the native roe deer (*Capreolus capreolus*) disappeared and was not reintroduced until 1730. Wild boar could be found in a few forests during Queen Elizabeth's time but their days were numbered. It is hard to believe that the sophisticated craft of the huntsman did not encompass some understanding of conservation; perhaps it did, but as things turned out, the tide of history was to prove overwhelming.

The Middle Ages were a time of great uncertainty. The twelfth and thirteenth centuries enjoyed a good climate with bountiful harvests. Fewer children died in infancy and the old grew rich and fat. As the population expanded comfortably, peasants cleared large areas of marginal land for agriculture. Churches and cathedrals were built as cities blossomed with wealth and culture. An army of woodcutters pushed back the margins of the great forests, opened up more roads for trade and founded new settlements where none had ever been before. Naturally, Europe's population of wolves dropped sharply.

Then, within a few years, everything was changed. Suddenly the climate took a turn for the worse. The years between 1314 and 1317 were miserably wet and

cold, with the result that harvests were ruined. Medieval corn was not so productive as our modern varieties. In those days a farmer would have planted one grain in order to harvest four. There was an immediate shortage of corn for seed, with the result that famine began to devastate Europe. Not far behind followed the diseases of pneumonia, bronchitis and influenza. Climatic uncertainty continued. The winter of 1335 – possibly the coldest of the millennium – brought further distress. As the Black Death swept along the new trade routes out of Asia, it must have seemed that the Grim Reaper himself stalked the streets. Certainly his macabre image is dominant in the art of the period. Over half the population of Europe died, between 25 and 45 percent victims of plague, the rest from privation and hunger. Some villages were so devastated that there was no one left to attend the corpses except wolves.

All across Europe thousands of starving people took to the roads. In the lawlessness that followed – compounded by the anarchy of the Hundred Years War – old fears took root once more. The occult practices of former times flourished again. Witches smeared with magic unguents rode broomsticks to satanic rendezvous; they were believed to walk abroad as wolves.

At the end of the Middle Ages, decimated by starvation and disease, the agricultural workers of Europe found themselves unable to farm in the traditional way. In many parts of Europe an acute shortage of labour allowed a great deal of farmland, particularly on the north German plain, to revert to forest. Sheep-farming became more important, for a single shepherd could manage hundreds of sheep with the help of only a few trained dogs. Of course, faced with this kind of encouragement, the wolf population bounced back, marauding domestic stock throughout France and Italy during the fourteenth and fifteenth centuries. Great fear swept France when reports of rabid wolves were circulated, and this led to a series of campaigns aimed at the extermination the wolf. It was to be a long battle.

The alleged werewolf of Eischenbach, Germany, (1685) falling into a well and being subsequently hanged. An engraving by George Jacob Schneider of Muremburg.

Der in seiner Menschlichen Wohnung noch
stets rasende des Verbannt: und gehangenen
so genanten: Menschen Wolffs; und.
Geist.

The sixteenth century werewolf of Eischenbach surprising one of its victims.

Fear of werewolves and witchcraft rose to hysteria-point towards the end of the sixteenth century. In 1598 a wave of prosecutions for lycanthropy (the transformation of a human being into a wolf) swept France, and the details were widely publicized throughout Europe. In the backroom of a tailor's shop in Châlons, France, a casket was discovered containing the bones of several children. We shall never know the satanic details, for it was ordered that the court records be destroyed when the lycanthrope was sentenced to death, but it was not an isolated case. In 1598 a whole family of werewolves was revealed in the Franche-Comté region. Pierre Gandillon, one of the accused, described attending a witches' sabbat: "Satan clothed them in a wolf's skin, which completely covered them, and that they went on all fours, and ran about the country, chasing now a person and now an animal according to the guidance of their appetite." Other cases followed, faithfully documented by Henri Boguet in one of the many demonologies published at the time. Led by self-styled witch-hunters, a wave of panic spread across the country and hundreds of executions were reported to have taken place. Eventually the cool head of French law prevailed.

The case of Jacques Roulet, a wild beggar caught feasting on the body of a fifteen-year-old boy, fed the public imagination with more images of horror. However, the case was referred to the Paris Parlement who discovered Roulet to be mentally deficient. They dismissed his "confession" that he had attended witches' sabbats and used a magic ointment to effect his transformation into a

As fear of the occult rose to hysteria during the sixteenth century, dread of werewolves or "wild men" was fueled by several cases which became notorious throughout Europe.

41

It is thought that wolves were extirpated from England by the year 1290, but a vigorous population survived in Scotland until the beginning of the eighteenth century. Many "last wolves" were reported from the Highlands. According to tradition, the very last one was killed in 1848.

wolf. His death sentence was commuted to two years' detention in the insane asylum of St Germain-des-Prés, where it was ordered that he was to receive religious instruction. In 1603 another boy was arrested. Under interrogation Jean Grenier plainly described how a man had given him a wolf-skin cape which, used in combination with a magic salve, transformed him into a wolf for about an hour at dusk. Grenier told of eating dogs but said, "Little girls taste better, their flesh is tender and sweet, their blood rich and warm." In spite of the diabolic nature of his fantasies, this boy was also humanely treated and sent to the seclusion of a monastery rather than to the stake. Never again would the courts recognize lycanthropy as a crime, but the peasants were not convinced. When wolf-hunts were organized in Franche-Comté during the 1650s, dread and argument broke out once again over the existence of werewolves.

The publication in 1486 of the *Malleus Maleficarum* by the German inquisitor Heinrich Kramer sparked off a series of malicious witch-hunts throughout Europe which continued to erupt in expressions of hysterical and self-righteous savagery for 200 years. Its victims (thousands of them) were predominantly female herbalists who harboured no arcane wolfish lusts whatsoever. Were-wolves are generally a male fantasy. Only a few cases of lycanthropy have ever been investigated and these point to mental derangement rather than any occult

A wolf from the Irish Book of Kells bears a demonic tail. The wolves of Ireland were said to be particularly large. Indeed, they may have been a subspecies that evolved during the Ice Age to hunt Irish Giant elk (moose).

cause. Nevertheless, the specter is alive and well in Europe to this day. A survey in 1992 showed that nearly 80 percent of Russian respondents still believed in werewolves.

These examples of witchcraft serve to highlight what was happening to the real wolves. On the European mainland their status was quite different to that in island Britain. It was not possible to eliminate every last wolf. The continent was too big, and the nature of wolf migration ensured that as soon as a pack was killed, new wolves would take over their territory within a short space of time. Nevertheless, some measures had to be taken to calm the superstitious peasants and to protect the revenues of their noble lords. In France, sometime between A.D. 800 and 813, the Emperor Charlemagne founded a special order to hunt wolves, known as the Louveterie. Paid out of government funds, members were also empowered to demand payment from all people living within a radius of two leagues from the place the wolf was killed. Not surprisingly, this led to the rapid eradication of the wolf from populated areas, but wolves in remote regions were left undisturbed.

Irish wolves were said to be particularly large. Perhaps they were a slightly more powerful subspecies that had evolved to kill Giant elk (moose). These super-wolves were particularly numerous between 1357 and 1387 and ordinances appeared, one after another, demanding their destruction. In 1652 Oliver Cromwell forbade the export of Irish wolfhounds – they were desperately needed at home – and legislation was passed offering generous bounties to wolf-hunters: 6 pounds was paid for a bitch, 5 pounds for a dog, 4 pounds for an independent cub and 10 shillings for a nursing pup. In the late seventeenth century wolves were still common. The writer John Dunton lodged at a farm in

A massive campaign against wolves in the United States, originally mounted by nineteenth-century settlers, resulted in their extirpation from most of the lower forty-eight states.

County Galway, where he was "strangely surprised to hear the cows and sheep all coming into my bed-chamber. I enquired the meaning and was told it was to preserve them from the wolf, which every night was rambling about for prey." The last wolf in Ireland was killed in 1821.

Wolf-hunting was a sport for the aristocracy in Russia.

In Scotland wealth depended on cattle, so wolves were the victims of strict hunting laws instigated during the second century B.C. by Dormadilla (or Djovadil), the fourth King of the Scots. It was decreed that the death of a wolf should be rewarded by the bounty of an ox. This handsome inducement did little to reduce the population in the long run, however. During the reign of James I, Scotland suffered from a plague of wolves which forced the King to pass laws instigating statutory hunts which all able-bodied men (with few exceptions) were obliged to attend. They took place between St. Mark's Day and Lammas (25 April and 1 August) so that pups as well as adults could be killed. The population of Scots wolves seems to have fluctuated wildly from decade to decade. During the reign of Mary, Queen of Scots, wolves were so numerous they were reported to be excavating churchyards. Although the statutory hunting laws ensured that every effort was made to stem their numbers, in the end it was not killing that finished off the Scots wolf but the wholesale destruction of their forest habitat by burning. The last wolf was probably killed sometime between 1690 and 1700, although there were many "last wolves," and Scots tradition held that the *very* last wolf was killed in 1848.

Years of steady attrition finally brought wolf-population numbers to critical levels all over Europe. In France, most packs had disappeared by 1800. The last

As overhunting by man destroyed populations of deer and wild boar throughout Europe and Asia, wolves found it hard to find natural prey.

individuals were killed in 1927 in Deux-Sèvres and in Haute-Vienne, although the Lieutenants de Louveterie still exist as an honored order to this day. In Central Europe the wolves disappeared as herds of deer and wild boar were devastated by organized hunting parties at the beginning of the nineteenth century. The last wolf in Denmark was killed in 1772, in Bavaria in 1847, and wolves were eliminated from the Rhineland – from Coblenza to the Saar – by 1889.

In Scandinavia the natural prey of wolves was the elk (moose), *Alces alces*. After centuries of overhunting, this large deer was temporarily extirpated in the nineteenth century by farmers who wanted to preserve all the grazing for the use of their domestic stock. Deprived of their natural food, hungry wolves began to harry cattle and domestic reindeer, which provoked a savage response. Thousands of people participated in synchronized drives to destroy the last wolves in northern Scandinavia. Although the elk has now been reintroduced, the wolf is still *persona non grata*. A few individuals have migrated into Scandinavia from Karelia but their existence has provoked a horrified outcry.

Attitudes seem to have been more relaxed in Italy and Spain, where rural shepherds had lived alongside wolves since antiquity. Although Kings Carlo VI and Francisco I organized a couple of large wolf-hunts, the mountainous terrain of much of central Italy defeated them. Landowners in Southern Europe tended to be city-dwellers who seldom visited their country estates anyway, except for a spot of deerhunting. Bounties were paid from the twelfth century up until 1950, but perhaps the authorities were too mean! The Italian wolf survived.

Kamala, one of the wolf children of Orissa, allegedly rescued by Reverend A. L. Singh. The photograph was taken in the 1920s.

Despite a seemingly endless catalogue of attempts to exterminate the species, wolves remained common over much of their European range up until the mid-nineteenth century. As in North America, numbers in Central Europe only began to drop when firearms and poisons became widely available. Within a few years they were virtually eliminated from most areas by these methods.

The Italian wolf expert, Dr Luigi Boitani, believes that Mediterranean people have accepted the presence of wolves more readily than their northern neighbors for cultural reasons. Among southern peasants who retain elements of pre-Christian faith in the form of superstition, the wolf represents the power of fertility as well as death. It is only in purely Christian cultures that we are confused by the two images. People of other beliefs, such as the Inuit of North America or the Indian devotees of the goddess Siva, might simply smile at the naivety of the idea that they were not indissolubly one.

The kindness of wolves is celebrated in scores of fables that celebrate their talent for parenthood. Romulus and Remus may have been a historical construct, but we now step out of the realm of mythology. Genuine feral children have turned up from time to time in every century. This is fact.

Five accounts of abandoned infants being cared for by animals were promoted in the eighteenth century by the philosopher Rousseau, who documented the stories in his *Discours sur l'Origine de l'Inégalité parmi les Hommes*. The subject fascinated the philosophers of the Enlightenment for the light it shed on the development of human qualities. Four years later, in 1758, the taxonomist

Linnaeus listed seven cases, adding three more when he reprinted the thirteenth edition of his *Systema Naturae* in 1782. He was so convinced of the veracity of the children that he subdivided his order of humans to include *Homo ferus*. By the end of the century, fourteen feral children had been recognized, several of them reputed to have been raised by wolves.

Although details differed, the children had certain features in common. For a start, few were initially grateful for their "rescue" from what must have been their substitute family. They showed fear. The children had no speech and it took years of patient care to teach them how to communicate their most basic needs. Feral children who appeared to have spent months – perhaps years – crouched in the confines of a den or running on all-fours, could not stand up or walk on two legs. They were carnivorous and refused to eat food other than raw meat.

In the oldest recorded case, that of the wolf-child of Hesse who was found running wild in the woods in 1344, the child made a remarkable mental recovery, although it was thought that he had been nurtured by wolves for as long as four years. Sadly, the progress achieved with most of the later children was limited. A Catholic priest, Father Erhardt reported that Dina Sanichar, the wolf-child captured near Mynepuri, India, in 1872, refused to wear clothes and persisted in gnawing bones to sharpen his teeth. Eventually he learned to dress with difficulty and to look after his own cup and plate.

The most complete description of wolf-children was made by an Indian pastor, the Reverend J. A. L. Singh, who ran an orphanage in Midnapore. His journal tells how on October 9, 1920, led by the villagers of Godamuri, Bengal, he found two girls in a wolves' den otherwise occupied by three adult wolves and two pups. The youngest child, named Amala by her rescuers, was roughly two years old, but her "sister" Kamala may have been eight. They had obviously been with the wolves for some time for they behaved like dogs, panting in the heat and (to everyone's horror) purposefully chasing chickens. They liked to root around in the household dump in search of carcasses and entrails and were seen to eat soil and pebbles. Their arrival clearly caused some turmoil in the Singh household, but the girls were carefully tended by Mrs Singh and detailed records describing their development were kept by her husband and a physician, Dr. Sarbadhicari. Amala died of kidney failure on September 12, 1921. Her sister survived eight years before, curiously, succumbing to the same disease. It took Kamala ten months to learn to use her hands to take food. Her joints were stiff, like those of all the other feral children reported over the centuries. Mrs Singh patiently massaged the child to allow extension of the leg, but it was five and a half years before she could walk, which she succeeded in doing in January 1926. Gradually her orientation changed and her intelligence improved. She had mastered a vocabulary of about fifty words before her death.

It has been suggested that the Reverend Singh did not, in fact, witness the exhumation of the children from the wolves' den. Perhaps he adjusted the dramatic story to include himself in a central role. Perhaps he needed some publicity to obtain money to run his little orphanage. Maybe the children were brought to him. In spite of these doubts, however, no one has ever questioned the existence of Amala and Kamala or the details contained in the orphanage records. Besides, Amala and Kamala were not the last wolf-children to be discovered in India.

Cycling through the forest of Musafirkhana near Sultanpur in 1972, a man called Narsingh Bahadur Singh came across several wolf cubs playing in the undergrowth in the company of a human child. This four-year-old vigorously resisted Narsingh's attempts to capture him, but eventually he was tied to the bicycle and taken to the village of Narayanpur. From 1972 until 1978 he was cared for by Narsingh's household. Then he was taken to Prem Nivas, Mother Theresa's Home for the Destitute and Dying in Lucknow, where he died in an emaciated condition seven years later.

The exposure of children to almost certain death seems to have been a traditional method of dealing with unwanted infants throughout Europe from antiquity. Although it has been suggested that this practice might "eliminate weaklings" to foster a super-race, the evidence indicates that the purpose was not to engender heroes. The theme of infant exposure is enshrined in the witchcraft of several European legends, notably the Babes in the Wood and Snow White and the Seven Dwarfs. These dark stories collected by the Brothers Grimm are only a representative handful from the folk tradition. Obviously, the idea of abandoning babies was not new. The killing of unwanted female babies remains endemic in modern India where the practice of demanding extortionate dowry payments often beggars families. This modern scandal is furthered by the abortion of female fetuses which are determined by electronic scan. Infanticide and abortion are now so widespread in India that it is thought the population may become unbalanced.

In the stories of wolves and abandoned children, the wolves appear as caring saviors which give the infants the nurturing that has been denied them by their natural parents. Of course, these tales – whether they are true or not – tell more about the mentality of humans than the behaviour of canids. But just for a moment . . . could wolves rear children? Is it possible?

As we shall see in the next chapter, the family life of wolves is highly social. Wolves act as members of a disciplined pack, not as individuals. Older members of the pack instinctively provide food for all the younger wolves, yearlings as well as pups, so the area of the den can be a busy feeding station for a large number of animals. But what about sucklings? And why are the wolves inhibited from eating the children?

Everyone has their theories, and this is mine: that there may be a "safety zone" around the den, a magic circle within which adult wolves are inhibited from making a kill. Working on this premise Red-breasted geese on the Taimyr peninsula in Russia deliberately build their nests and rear their young close by the nests of peregrine falcons. The falcon's strongest instinct is to defend its territory from Arctic foxes, Snowy owls and other predators. It totally ignores the goose and her tasty little goslings, who benefit from the protection of a bird that in other circumstances they would seek to avoid. We know that, like falcons, foxes are inhibited from killing their immediate neighbours. Wolves and foxes are close relatives. If the strongest instinct of the wolf in the general area of the den is to nurture and feed, perhaps that instinct may override all others, allowing the human infant to survive.

CHAPTER FOUR

SHARING AND CARING

This is a no-nonsense system of reproduction that forges strong,
competent animals. Life is generally tough for wolves.

L. David Mech, *The Way of the Wolf* (Swan Hill Press, 1992)

The tender rearing of offspring is one of the cornerstones of wolf behavior, one of the main reasons for the wolf's success as a species. Wolf parents seem to raise their pups with exemplary attention, but it is in fact a group effort which starts as soon as the dominant or alpha female has selected the site of the den. This might be a traditional birthplace, used by wolves for hundreds of years. Or it could be a hole freshly excavated beneath the roots of a tree. Some dens are dug amidst the shelter of boulders, in a place that is safe from disturbance and easy to defend. As the birth draws imminent, the alpha female goes to ground while the pack rallies round in support. The entire pack, not just the alpha male, cooperates to bring food to sustain her while she suckles the newborn pups.

The pups are born into a family of caring parents and tail-wagging aunts and uncles. In the dark safety of the den, they are suckled for the first four weeks by a mother who hardly leaves them for a moment. She must stay constantly with the pups if they are to survive, for they are unable to regulate the heat of their own bodies to begin with and need the warmth of their mother's coat if they are not to die from cold. While she is occupied with caring, food is left by other pack members at the entrance to the den. At three weeks of age the pups' eyes open, and the strongest staggers towards the mouth of the den to emerge for the first time into daylight. Now the whole pack joins in feeding and rearing the new generation. The size of the litter varies: normally between four and seven pups are born, but litters of up to thirteen have been recorded.

Between six and nine weeks of age, the pups are weaned. By this time the neighborhood of the den has a distinctly well-used look about it. The grass is soiled and trampled and there are traces of many wolf feasts lying about, so it is quite smelly. Hygiene is probably low on the wolves' list of priorities, but they may be concerned that the den is conspicuous, so the pups are moved to a new place to be used as a rendezvous site. Again, this is sometimes in forested undergrowth or in the shelter of a pile of rocks; sometimes it is a circular playpen made amongst tall grasses. The rendezvous site functions like a den – but above ground.

As soon as the pups are weaned, the adults return to normal hunting activities and may return to feed them only once every couple of days. The hunters use their stomachs like a bag to carry the meat back to the den. Their arrival is heralded with yelps of excitement, the pups falling over each other to jump up at the mouths of the older wolves which stimulates them to regurgitate the partly digested meat. Wolves can pack away a huge amount of food in their stomachs, as the phrase "wolf it down" indicates. Adults may regurgitate up to three times and still have plenty of meat left to satisfy themselves.

The juveniles of the pack keep the pups company; they bring them a share of their own small kills and play with them while their parents are away. This is not entirely altruistic. These subadult yearlings get a substantial share of whatever prey the adult wolves bring back, so it is in their interests to hang about the den. Some spend up to 50 percent of their time babysitting. It's worth it. When the adults make a large kill, the juveniles are ready to backtrack the scent of their trail and lay claim to part of the carcass. Although the pups are never short of playmates, the juveniles take a large share of the food brought back to the den. In times of hardship, this means that the pups die first.

Occasionally a large animal is killed quite close to the den, in which case the parents will fetch the youngsters to the carcass. The pups can travel up to a mile from the den by the time they are five or six weeks old. The whole pack will gorge and sleep around the kill for several days, until the bones are picked clean. Afterwards they may not bother to go back to the den, from then on using the site of the kill as the new rendezvous.

The pups find themselves on the bottom rung of the pack's hierarchical ladder. They are loved and cared for by everyone, but they are continually reminded of their true social standing as well. Every pack member plays with the pups, teasing them and rolling them in the dust when they get too excited. In this way the youngsters gain physical coordination as they sort out the niceties of social behavior in the friendly mafia into which they have been born. Among themselves, a tussle for dominance is already taking place that will have far-reaching effects. The cosy body contact of the young wolves at rest explodes into bouts of wrestling, running play, nipping and biting. Even now, it's obvious which are the strongest and most likely to survive the next winter. The boldest take the most food and gain bodyweight more quickly. Thrusting, rolling, running and chewing turn their puppyfat into muscle.

Wolves love to play. Even as adults they never quite grow out of it. Younger wolves sometimes react in an impulsive way to interesting objects they find while travelling. A piece of animal hide might be towed about, or a bone flung up in the air and chased. Low-ranking wolves, hanging around the rendezvous site, play not only with the pups but boisterously among themselves. Although they are not mature, a distinct sexual division is acknowledged. Once past the puppy stage, young males do not usually play with females, they are only interested in the power struggle with each other.

Playful behavior (the kind of silly antics your pet dog might indulge in just before you feed him) can act to defuse a potentially aggressive situation. A juvenile might bounce around a little, then lower its body and playfully raise a paw as a friendly appeasement gesture to soothe the beta or alpha male. Females play among themselves, but not to quite the same extent as males. They do not seem to use frivolity to deflect aggression, perhaps because they know that if the

Previous page: The alpha female chooses the site of the maternity den, and this usually determines the hunting territory of the entire pack for several months, while they raise the pups cooperatively.

alpha female is annoyed, she will press home her attack regardless. For wolves, play is a serious occupation since it is out of the spontaneous joie de vivre of young wolves that the complex social behavior of adulthood develops.

For the pack is a group of wolves held together by a curious mixture of rigid behavior patterns spiced with individual opportunity and waywardness. In other words, it's a family, bonded by ties of caring similar to those which humans call love. This subtle web of relationship offers the pups their best chance of survival. If the mother wolf had to rear her offspring unaided, she would be hard-pushed to find enough food near the den to keep the family from starvation. Most of her pups would die. For adult wolves, the pack provides the opportunity to cooperate with others in hunting, an advantage which enables them to bring down larger prey than they could do alone. Big groups also enable the pack to defend their kill from competitors such as bears and they allow wolves to establish and defend large territories.

Supported by the pack, the young wolves can afford to grow up slowly, learning as they mature. It may be several years before a young wolf gains sufficient savvy, strength or status to breed, but the time spent in the birth-pack is not wasted. Wolves who have helped their mother rear brothers and sisters may learn the tricks and traps of parenthood. In this way, when they become parents

Soon after their eyes are opened, the pups emerge from the den to meet the rest of the pack.

The female wolf keeps her pups warm with the heat from her own body during their first few days of life, when they are unable to regulate their own temperature.

themselves, they are experienced and therefore more likely to be successful. Some wolves never achieve families of their own, however, for there is only room for so many packs within an environment and wolves take care to regulate their own numbers very strictly.

A wolf-pack normally consists of an alpha male and female with their offspring, perhaps the product of several seasons. Packs like this can remain stable for many years, but from time to time events occur which compromise the situation. Hunting by man causes tremendous disturbance, for when wolves are killed, established social relationships break down. The pack may split up, later re-forming to incorporate new members. Packs vary in size from seven to twenty members, depending on the size of prey they specialize in hunting. Wolves in Southern Europe are often solitary. They have no need for complex social organization because they rely on small prey like hares and rodents and they only

pair to breed. In the Arctic, by comparison, where wolves depend on caribou (wild reindeer) and musk-oxen to see them through the winter, social organization is essential.

The bonds that hold a wolf-pack together are very strong. The alpha male and female represent two distinct lineages of power which seldom overlap. No one can say who really leads the pack, for the top male and female seem to share the responsibility. They both maintain power by suppressing the sexuality of the younger wolves of their own sex. The alpha male prevents other males from gaining access to the alpha female during her estrus, while the alpha female bullies the younger females, her rivals, into a state of sexless immaturity which persists regardless of biological age. As a result, only the top dogs breed. That is the theory, at any rate. Wolf-packs have a habit of confounding biologists with atypical behavior every once in a while. Sometimes a lower-ranking female produces a litter. Sometimes a pack produces two litters. Sometimes an alpha female mates with a lower-ranking male when the alpha male isn't looking. All sorts of things can happen, particularly when the social relationships between the wolves are disturbed by the death – or the aging – of one of the alpha team.

The alpha wolves share a close monogamous relationship which may persist for many years but is not necessarily a bond for life. For one reason or another, either male or female may be usurped by a younger member of the pack. The position of leader is held as the result of a campaign of intimidation which goes on throughout the year, male and female demonstrating their dominance over their own sex in ritual ways that demand continual submission. Further down

Farmers and native hunters have a tradition of controlling wolf numbers by removing pups from the den each spring. Although distasteful, in areas where wolf control is considered essential, killing pups may cause less disturbance to the social order of the pack than hunting.

the line, the beta wolves of secondary rank are demanding recognition from the juveniles, and in their turn the juveniles are teaching respect to the new pups.

Serious fighting may lead to injury and the incapacity of a key member of the pack, so most of the antagonism is played out in displays of body language. One way a wolf can dominate another of close rank is by staring him down. To emphasize the tactic it might sidle up alongside, holding its legs and back rigid and its tail extended stiffly behind. Growling and raising its hackles, the dominant wolf will try to make the other withdraw or adopt a submissive posture.

Submissive behaviour is what keeps the peace throughout the pack. Alpha wolves expect to receive it from every pack member, but the rest give and receive submissive signals depending on their status. It does not seem to be a regime of terror, however. Subservient wolves in the middle of the pack-structure appear as though they are happy to reassure the leadership, to reinforce the bonds of friendly relationship. At their own level of dominance, they are exchanging signals among themselves, so the balance of power in the pack is not static but always open to the exciting possibility of change. Only the omega wolf looks unhappy. Omega is Greek for "last" and, as one would expect, this wolf "gets it in the neck" from everyone.

Some of the submissive displays arise from the behavior of pups. Sticking out its tongue, the submissive wolf may try to lick the alpha wolf's mouth in a parody of a puppy begging for food. It whines while lowering its body to the ground in a beseeching gesture that reminds the older wolf of the kindliness due to the young. While the alpha wolf stands over the subdominant animal, with its ears pricked up, tail and hackles raised, the subservient wolf looks up at the top dog – and then looks away in exaggerated formality. It lowers its body and thrusts its tail between its legs, at the same time flattening its ears and pulling its lips back into a "grin" of appeasement. The junior wolf might even crawl forward on its belly in a gesture of pure abasement, rolling over to expose its genitals to the mercy of the dominant alpha.

Sometimes the beta wolf proves troublesome and simply refuses to oblige with the required pantomime. This is a real challenge to the domestic order of the pack, a threat to the status quo. The dominant wolf must insist on submission, perhaps by standing on its back legs and putting its paws on the other wolf's shoulders. Accompanied by a rumble of growling, the alpha will pretend to bite its adversary, play-acting what will happen if the offender doesn't back down.

The alpha wolf may hold power for several years but eventually the day comes when the beta wolf senses that the older animal is weakening. Perhaps it is some small injury that makes the leader vulnerable. Now the beta wolf risks everything by instigating a serious battle. This time they bite for real, seizing fur and skin between their teeth, shaking their heads to tear each other's flesh. A serious fight is deeply disturbing for the other wolves in the pack. They may wander around whining and making submissive gestures as if to keep the peace. When neither protagonist will back down, it will turn into a fight to the death. If the alpha wolf – whether male or female – is defeated, it will lose all rank within the pack. Transformed from alpha to omega (and probably injured too) the deposed wolf must ingratiate itself with the pack members that it once commanded. Continually chivvied by the other adults, life may become so uncomfortable that it is forced to leave its family and spend the rest of its life subsisting alone.

Submissive behaviour keeps the peace within the pack. Subdominant wolves seldom raise their tails in the presence of the alpha leader.

The social hierarchy of males and females is separate and independent, so males do not challenge or fight females. However, the alpha female is not shy when it comes to confrontation. She is usually the fiercest member of the pack and her intimidation of the other females is relentless. Many of the low-ranking females keep clear of her altogether, following the pack at a respectful distance to pick up scraps from the kill when the top female has eaten her fill. Physically smaller than males, low-ranking females may be reluctant to leave the pack unless they are confident of making a living on their own. In areas where the wolves depend on large prey like musk-oxen or moose (European elk), cooperative hunting is important. Unless they are unusually powerful, the females must put up with the aggravation until they have matured enough to confront the alpha bitch physically. That could take years.

Given a few good seasons, a wolf-pack can outgrow its territory. Young wolves usually spend their first winter hunting with the pack. They have got a lot to learn and it's their best chance of survival. The next spring and summer they spend more time alone or in the company of other youngsters hunting small prey. They are practising independence. Leaving the pack is probably the last thing a wolf wants to do, but if the all-powerful alpha wolves are young, their offspring will never get a chance to breed. Low-ranking female wolves show by their estrus that they are mature sexually and capable of bearing pups, but somehow the psychological dominance of the alpha female suppresses the urge to mate. If the alpha male shows interest in a low-ranking female, the alpha female usually

Above: A Spanish wolf signals its submission by adopting a helpless, playful posture.

Excitement runs high in a captive wolf-pack during the mating season. While the alpha leaders are tied in copulation and unable to drive him away, a subdominant male attempts to join in.

After a few weeks the area around the den gets soiled so the pack moves to a rendezvous site, which acts as a centre for their activities through the summer. These are Arctic wolves.

responds by attacking her mercilessly, perhaps driving her out of the pack. If she mates and conceives, the alpha female is likely to kill her pups.

The alpha wolf is not defending monogamy. Although she usually prefers the alpha male (who is strong and a good hunter), given a chance she will mate with the beta wolf or indeed any male wolf who takes her fancy. The alpha male tries to dominate his subordinates so that they are afraid to mate with her, even if she tempts them. The pack offers security and a square meal, but nothing else. As a wolf matures it must make a life or death decision. To stay with the pack and live, or to risk everything for the small chance of establishing its own pack and founding a new genetic line.

It is a move that is fraught with danger, for it is only inside the boundary of its own pack's territory that an individual is safe from attack by other wolves. The moment it leaves, it will have to run a gauntlet of aggression until it finds a place of its own. A lone wolf may be killed straight away by the neighboring pack. Unable to bring down large prey animals unaided, the lone wolf may become physically weak and vulnerable. It might just starve to death. On leaving the

Although dominance and submission are the social glue which holds the pack together, there is plenty of playful good feeling too.

pack, the loner tends to strike out quickly, sometimes travelling more than 100 miles (161 km) in a straight line, as though to get away from home as fast as possible. Gambling with the unknown, the lone wolf must sense that somewhere there is a female willing and ready to breed with him and that together they will succeed in carving out for themselves a hunting territory.

He shortens the odds by leaving a trail of scent down the edge of all the wolf territories he passes through. This may seduce some low-ranking female into breaking with her pack to take the same enormous gamble. If a male lone wolf finds a promising piece of territory, he settles into it, hunting for himself and keeping a lookout for lone females. They do turn up sometimes, although the urge to migrate seems to be less ardent. Sometimes, as we have seen, the alpha female in the birth-pack is so aggressive that a young female is literally driven out. Small clues lead her in the same direction as other travelers. Finally she reaches a place where scent marks tell her to stay for a while, or better still, to howl for company. Lone wolves have an uncanny knack of sniffing each other out. In 1982 the only male wolf in Scandinavia managed to find the only female wolf.

CHAPTER FIVE

WILD, UNTAMED MUSIC

They float at the edge of things; between a walk and a run, between light and dark. At the extremity of the forest they linger invisible as shadows, for the wolf is as much a genius of stillness as of movement.

Cutting through the crisp air of a winter's evening, a single howl rises above the trees. It is a primeval cry from the earth and it never fails to elicit that special stab of astonishment which causes the hairs to prickle on the back of one's neck. Gaining energy, the call rises, sonorous with harmonics, hanging for long seconds in the darkness before starting to fade. As the sound dies away, a second voice joins in, a polite contralto following the opening solo. It's on the same bearing; the two wolves are together. Then, coming from a quite different direction this time, a crescendo of wails echoes down the valley as a whole pack gives voice. After a few moments all is quiet. A hush settles over the wood, a profound silence as though all nature were holding its breath. Rimed with frost, the grass crackles softly underfoot. Out of the shadows a line of wolves emerges, moving one by one into the moonlight.

Howling plays an important part in the lives of wolves. It is an outward sign of the cohesion of the wolf-pack, a celebration of what they are. Wolves appear to howl for pleasure. It makes them feel good to have their clan gathered round, making a noise. It cements social bonds within the group, reminding each wolf that he (or she) is more than an individual, part of something large and hugely important, an honoured member of a pack. Yet this cannot be all there is to know about howling, because the smaller subspecies of wolf, *Canis lupus pallipes* and *Canis lupus arabs*, which live in the warmer climates of Iran, Iraq and Israel, do not howl very much if, at all. It has been suggested that this may be because desert nights are often windy and the howl of a wolf cannot be heard by other wolf packs. Or it may be that persecution by man has led them to suppress their natural cries.

During the early summer months, even northern wolves howl very little. Activity is centred around the den and rendezvous sites, so they see all the other pack members nearly every day. In the autumn the pack often splits up and the wolves may hunt in ones and twos. At this time of year a good howl comes in useful to find out where the main body of the family has got to.

Wolves howl more frequently during the winter and in early spring. Lone migrant wolves howl to make contact with others and to find a mate.

Previous page: Wolves occasionally travel alone, but they are constantly on the look out for others. Intensely sociable animals, wolves depend on communication as well as cooperation to make a living.

When winter starts in earnest, the wolves gather together, cooperating to make the big kills they need to see them through the hard months. In Denali National Park, Alaska, wolves take caribou, moose and Dall sheep. Further south, their prey is white-tailed or black-tailed deer. In northern Russia wolves rely on reindeer and elk, which are simply caribou (*Rangifer tarandus*) and moose (*Alces alces*) by another name. However the prey is described, wherever the wolves happen to be, these are the crucial months.

When a wolf-pack gives voice, neighboring packs often howl right back, as if to say, "OK, well, if you are *there*, then we are *here*." This immediate response helps to define the territories of both packs by establishing areas of dominance. However, it also tells the next-door pack precisely where the action is. An aggressive alpha wolf might use this information to lead its pack on a lightning raid right into the heart of next-door's territory, secure in the knowledge that the resident pack is occupied elsewhere. Perhaps for this reason, wolves do not

always choose to reply to the howling of their neighbors.

Although howling helps to establish a sense of territory, the wolves are not trying to intimidate each other. Humans might find the sound a little scary, but for wolves howling is undoubtedly interesting, even alluring. In the past it was thought that the long relationship between the two alpha wolves and their sexual dominance of the rest of the pack must cause inbreeding, but it seems that the integrity of the wolf-pack is not absolute. Wolf-packs exchange members from time to time; just often enough to allow genetic variability. Occasionally the whole pack may break up and re-form. Howling surely plays a part in this essential correspondence.

Wolves always react to howling in some way, although they give a vocal reply less than 50 percent of the time. Sometimes they set off towards the sound, perhaps with the intention of investigation. Sometimes their neighbors' howling seems to annoy them, and has been known to precipitate a direct attack. Where the density of wolves is very high and there is competition for dwindling food supplies, this is a significant danger. The movement of deer in winter encourages packs in Superior National Forest, Minnesota, to invade each other's territories regularly, and it is known that wolves are often killed on these excursions. If an alpha wolf dies, the disruption to the social order is so severe that the pack may scatter, leaving its territory in the possession of the invaders.

So wolves do not howl all through the night as they beat the bounds of their territory. They may give voice only once in ten hours, perhaps at dawn or dusk.

Both urine and faeces carry interesting messages. Here, the members of a captive pack sniff at the alpha female's urine on the ground, while she and her mate copulate on the right.

Although the harmonies in the wolf-song act to confuse the listener, there's no doubt that wolves can read a great deal between the lines. This information may be dangerous to the established social order of the pack. A virile beta wolf might work out the age and strength of the alpha in a neighbouring pack and reckon his chances to mate there to be stronger than within his own pack. An "outcast" female might flee her over-assertive mother to risk a new life among strangers.

Although there are drawbacks to advertising, howling clearly fulfills a deep need within the wolf-pack. There may not be a single purpose; wolves may howl for a variety of reasons, including anxiety and unrest. Pups howl when they are left alone by their mother. If they get lost, they howl until some member of the pack finds them. Captive wolf pups moved out of their familiar surroundings for a period of eight hours, howled without pause for six of them. Once, during a serious fight for dominance between two senior wolves, the lower-ranking females were seen to run about distractedly, howling in distress.

As sexual activity within the pack quickens during January and February, howling increases into a regular activity most commonly performed in the early morning and late afternoon. The group choruses last longer and the number of solo performances increases. As the time for copulation approaches, social tension within the pack winds up, and aggressive altercations between the alpha male and female and their subordinates become more frequent. It is at this point

that low-ranking wolves, who have no hope of mating within the family, begin to consider striking out on their own.

The lone wolf is at a tremendous disadvantage when exploring new country. If it runs into a hostile pack it may be killed immediately. Fortunately wolf territories are laid out to be read like a road map, marked at every turn with olfactory signposts. Wolves are continually scent-marking wherever they go, for their paws leave a continuous light trace of scent which can be detected by other wolves for at least three days. However, they also leave scats – which stay smelly longer – in a continuous trail along regularly used routes. Like dogs, wolves have scent glands just inside the anus. As the sphincter muscles contract to expel the feces, a powerful secretion laden with pheromones is also expelled. This "calling card" is as individual as a fingerprint and much more interesting – to canids anyway. Wolves leave a scat about every 250 yards along well-used routes. Every 400 yards or so the pack will pause to spray landmarks such as rocks and tree-stumps with urine, which is also laden with personal information in complex

A female wolf in season urinates near an interested male.

Wolf scent builds up along well-used trails, guiding this European wolf through the mountains.

chemical form. The alpha wolves show their superiority by raising their legs to urinate. The others stand or squat.

As wolves tend to use the same paths all the time, with only occasional diversions for the purpose of hunting or taking short cuts, the burden of scent on the trail becomes quite pronounced. Wolves scent-mark more profusely around the edges of their territories where there is usually an overlap of roughly half a mile (1 km) with the area dominated by the neighboring pack. So when a strange wolf comes into the vicinity it can smell precisely where the edge of the two territories lies. Both packs use this fringe, although not at the same time, so one would expect this to be a dangerous place, but in fact it is quite the opposite! It is here that the interloper is most secure, for if it is chased by one pack it can escape into the domain of the other to throw off its pursuers. Independent wolves are not alone in working out this strategy. During the winter, deer are frequently found clumped together for safety in the "gray area" between wolf territories.

Naturally the lone wolf will leave its own olfactory signs wherever it goes.

When the resident pack next visits the area, these traces, together with those of the neighboring wolf-pack which may have passed through in the previous few days, will excite a lot of interest. The wolves will sniff the scats, perhaps even licking the urine marks for a finer appreciation. Then they will leave their own scent on top. They may follow the tracks of their rivals back into the next-door territory, just a few hundred yards usually, although they sometimes risk a deeper incursion if they think they can get away with it.

Although a powerful band of scent delineates the edge of the territory, the pack is not imprisoned by this boundary and frequently crosses it. The scent-marks are primarily a means of communication between wolves who cannot afford to meet face to face, and the knowledge learned from listening to their neighbors allows them to make sensitive adjustments to the size of their territory from time to time. Scent-marks are reassuring if they are your own, exciting if they belong to someone else. They may also act as reminders. Within each territory there will be "hotspots" of scent around the site of old kills. These are important places, for wolves with good memories may repeat the success of one season again the following year.

Wolves are incorrigible travellers. They are always on the move, checking up on the whereabouts of prey. Although most of their journeys are less than 3 miles (5 km), they can probably get right round their territory in the space of three weeks. This is not in any sense a patrol, for wolves do not actively guard their hunting grounds. When they find a really promising area they settle down there for a few days. They don't seem to care that the rest of the territory is lying "undefended."

No one has yet worked out how to read the subtle aromas imbued in wolf scats and urine, but we can read messages in the places where the scats are found. They show where wolves like to go, and how they get there. Droppings tell us that wolves will take the easiest path, using forest trails, footpaths and even main roads to get about. That is why they are sometimes traffic casualties.

Wolves often use human trails, particularly when snow is deep and difficult to walk through. It was reported that one wolf researcher, engaged in trailing a pack by snowmobile, was humbled to discover that the wolves had doubled back and were now trailing him, quietly making use of the compacted snow left by his vehicle. Wolves are certainly shrewd and seldom let a good opportunity such as this go by. Nevertheless, they are generally shy animals, with a deep fear of man that is far greater than their fear of other wolves. The footpaths of Isle Royale National Park in Michigan are thick with wolf feces in winter. When snow is on the ground, the wolves very sensibly use the man-made paths to get from one good hunting ground to another. As soon as human backpackers arrive in the spring, they change their habits to avoid the trails.

In spite of the timidity of the wolf, thousands of human wolf enthusiasts have succeeded in making contact with wild packs by going out into the wilderness to howl themselves. The response is extraordinary. Although the wolves must be able to tell the difference – they must know this is their arch enemy calling – they often respond energetically with howls of their own. What can they be saying? The groups of enthusiasts who flock to spend a night under the stars listening to the wild music of wolves are in no doubt of the meaning of this exchange. It touches their hearts. They return home carrying something rare and precious, a first-hand contact with wild wolves and nature.

CHAPTER SIX

WOLVES AND THEIR PREY

*"I now know how a live prey must feel. The wolves chase it until it is
tired, they bite at it, using the canine teeth as anchors so that a secure
grip can be made before the jaws are closed. The head shake embeds the
teeth farther into the body and each bite renders the prey less and less
able to retaliate or to escape because of the crush wounds. Slash wounds
inflicted by the canine teeth would cause less severe or immediate
damage than the crush wounds, which result in extensive muscle and
tendon injury and impairment of movement."*

Michael W. Fox describing how he felt when attacked by captive wolves
in his book *The Behaviour of Wolves, Dogs and Related Canids*
(Jonathan Cape, 1971)

Caribou, the wild reindeer of North America, spend the coldest part of the winter
in the south of their range among the trees of the taiga, where they huddle
together in assemblies known as "deer yards." Here they find shelter from the
Arctic wind and get a little warmth from the trunks of the trees which retain a
slight residual glow. The herd scrapes at the ground with their shovel-like feet to
expose the lichens on which they feed. Bodies packed tight together, they lose less
heat to the environment, and this strategy also helps to protect them from the
predators. Wolves are the caribou's constant companions. With hunger gnawing
at their bellies, they are eager to make a kill, but hundreds of deer eyes are on
guard and it is not easy to pick off a victim.

Although the weather remains bitterly cold and spring is still several weeks
away, the caribou get restless as the days begin to lengthen. Migration is a matter
of precise timing. A fidgety spirit seizes them as they instinctively respond to
millions of years of evolutionary pressure. They must give birth in the right place,
at the right time, so that their young will be weaned at precisely the right moment
to benefit from the succulent shoots and long days of an Arctic summer. Those
that don't will die.

The herds join together in a stream of continually moving animals. With the
first hatch of flies – which is equally carefully timed – the pace speeds up. Lashed
by mosquitoes and warble-flies, the caribou run for sanctuary into the frigid
north, pursued by clouds of biting insects. Sometimes ahead, sometimes running
in their wake, come the wolves.

While some wolves choose to hold on to their territories in the forested taiga regions, others migrate with the caribou to establish dens and hunting territories further north near the calving grounds. Arctic wolves, residents of the far north who subsist in the most extreme conditions all the year round, are generally paler than their southern cousins, sometimes white. A distinct subspecies, they are physically larger too. Big animals are better able to regulate their internal temperature than small creatures in cold climates because their surface area to body-mass ratio is lower and they lose less body heat to the environment.

Where the taiga thins into birch scrub and open country, light snowfall enables human observers to track the wolves from aircraft. A bird's-eye view shows the delicate tracery of their footprints. The temporary impression of their hunting strategy fans outward in long arcs that form perfect semi-circles around the thrust of the caribou's migration. The wolves are doing what dogs like to do best. They are herding the caribou, controlling their onward rush. Now and again they gather to separate an individual from the horde. They kill, and for a few hours there is a respite from hunger.

The Gray wolf can be found in an astonishing variety of habitats, from the Negev desert of Israel to the mountains of Greece but the taiga is its stronghold in both North America and Russia. Wolves avoid the denser parts of the forest where snow builds up to lie a yard or more deep. They hunt more effectively in forest clearings and on the edge of the taiga where the snow has blown away or become compacted. The most sought-after denning areas lie on the northern edge of the tree-line, within strike of the caribou for most of the year.

Although the wolf-pack can lope along at a steady 5 or 6 miles (8 or 9 km) per hour, they cannot outdistance their prey in sprint. Caribou can run at speeds of up to 40 miles (64 km) per hour, whilst wolves can barely manage 35 miles (56 km). If they are to eat, they must take other factors into account in planning their hunting strategy. The terrain is of crucial importance. As young wolves get familiar with their pack's territory, they realize that some places are good for kills while others favor the escape of the prey. On steep slopes goats and wild sheep will skip out of reach, seeking shelter on the top of knife-edged ridges or dangerous cliffs. Here wolves must hesitate to go. Instead, they will try to panic the prey into falling.

The prey's immediate reaction to attack gives the wolves a very good idea of how the hunt will unfold and whether it is worth the chase. Sheep or goats that run uphill are usually ignored. They are clearly fit and robust, and it is a waste of energy to pursue them, but an animal that runs downhill is another matter. It is obviously lacking in vitality and may be sick or starved. Running downhill, a panic-stricken individual is likely to trip and break a limb before it reaches security. It is easy meat.

Wolves like their prey to be vulnerable in some way because hunting is an exhausting business. Wolves are subtle accountants. The "energy budget" that each pack can afford to spend on the hunt depends on how many calories they will come out ahead after the "burn" of the chase. Wolves watch their prey – sometimes for days – before making a move. They notice the individuals that seem to be feeding less well, those whose stiff movements indicate age and arthritis. These are the animals they target, but even wolves make mistakes. Sometimes the pack starts to hunt and then, for no apparent reason, gives up. Some small detail suggests failure. Rather than waste precious energy, they call off the chase.

Previous page: Carnivores at the apex of the food chain, wolves depend on a healthy, balanced environment for their survival.

The hunt itself lasts only a few minutes, but wolves are really hunting all the time, watching to identify the individual they can kill with least cost to themselves. Usually that means they are focussing on the sick and the elderly, the newly born and the injured, but quirks in the climate can result in perfectly fit animals falling prey to wolves. Although moose (European elk), *Alces alces*, are strong enough to bulldoze their way through most snowdrifts, they can get bogged down in icy mud. Sudden deep snowfalls can trap smaller deer – particularly the semidomestic reindeer of Eurasia – leaving them vulnerable. In situations like this, the wolf-pack may kill several animals. A sharp freeze often leaves a crust of ice, several centimetres thick, lying over the snow. This favors wolves who dart across the surface without breaking through, but moose find the going arduous as their legs plunge through the ice into the soft snow beneath. They are at a disadvantage, and that is as dangerous to strong animals in their prime as it is to the frail.

During the summer, moose sometimes escape the wolf-pack by wading into deep water. Wolves can swim if they must, but they cannot chase moose doing the doggy-paddle. Instead they hang around the shallows waiting for the moose to come ashore. In winter, it is a different matter. The lakes are frozen. Driven on to the ice, the moose's feet slip from under them and they cannot defend themselves with the violent kicks they would normally employ on land. Even the strongest animal will die if the pack catches it in the wrong place.

Clever use of terrain is the wolf's stock-in-trade. That is the whole point of those checking and driving movements on migration. They put the herd under continual pressure, so the caribou are pushed to cross habitats they might otherwise avoid. There is safety in numbers, plenty of eyes watching for danger, so the wolves try to divide the herd into smaller groups. Every now and again the weakest pauses or a healthy animal makes a tactical error. Sensitive to the smallest indication of faltering, the wolves prosecute another kill.

Large prey is particularly important in winter when low temperatures mean that animals must burn precious calories just keeping warm. Although the youngest wolves may have spent the summer months successfully hunting lemmings, voles and snowshoe hares, they must now compete with hungry lynx and fox for what's left of the small mammal population. It is not enough. They must learn to hunt like adults.

Hunting prowess is a matter of courage, skill and judgment. Mastery must be acquired by watching and imitating, a process that needs the experience of several seasons. The pack learns to work together, each contributing according to age and ability. A study on Isle Royale, Michigan, showed that out of a pack consisting of fifteen wolves, only six of them physically attacked the prey. The rest devoted themselves to chasing, chivvying and watching. Although alpha wolves tend to be in the lead, social position means nothing in the hunt, and low-ranking animals do not hang back. Surprise is not important to success, but speed definitely matters. Lightly built young females make excellent hunters because they can run extremely fast in long encircling arcs that surround the prey, and prevent escape, but they may lack the strength to bring large animals down. Adult males are slower but more powerful, better equipped to knock moose or caribou to the ground with a timely blow to the shoulder. Precision is essential, for those flailing hooves can kill. When the pack has separated out and surrounded its victim, the wolves usually bite the hind leg and flank. Although

An alpha wolf shows its dominance by raising its tail.

these bites do not necessarily draw much blood, they cause massive muscle damage and shock. While half the pack harries the victim from the rear, a courageous wolf dives in to seize the prey by its nose. It holds tight. Big cats have jaws and teeth designed to suffocate their victims. They go for the throat. Wolves are not equipped to kill quickly in this way. Death sometimes takes many minutes and is caused by shock and hemorrhage. The wolf's style seems distressingly brutal, but profound shock caused by the nose-hold brings the attack closer to its conclusion.

The alphas eat first and then the other wolves join in the feast with their permission. One or two of the lowest-ranking members of the pack may hang back, and clearly, when times are hard, it is the omega wolf that starves. Generally, when there is enough meat to go round, everyone gets a bellyful, which can be up to 20 pounds (9 kg) at one sitting. After gorging, the wolves stagger away to sleep and digest, but they do not go far. They must defend their hard-won carcass from foxes, wolverines and lynx, not to mention other wolves. The raven seems to enjoy a special relationship with wolves, which allow this

intelligent scavenger to pick among the bones. Sometimes bears get a scent of the meat and come down to fight the wolves for a share of the kill, and occasionally wolves harass bears when they have brought down prey. A big carcass will keep the entire pack well fed for several days. The scraps will disappear overnight to others who watch and wait.

Often the size of the wolf-pack is related to the species of the prey. Arctic wolves who depend on musk-oxen may need a large pack of up to twenty to make a kill. Shoving the calves into the middle of the herd, musk-oxen form a defensive circle around them, bristling with lowered horns and heavy brows. The ring is impenetrable as long as it holds, so the wolves must entice it to break. The boldest run at the musk-oxen's horns, teasing and taunting them to chase. Sometimes they do. While the herd is thus occupied, the rest of the wolf-pack dives into the mêlée to chase off a tasty juvenile. An adult male musk-ox can weigh up to 1,430 pounds (650 kg), but there's plenty of meat on a youngster to satisfy a pack of wolves.

To bring down large deer usually requires the combined efforts of the whole pack. A moose (European elk) is a formidable animal which can weigh over 770 pounds (350 kg). It is not slow to attack its tormentors with well-aimed kicks and tosses from its huge antlers. If the moose stands its ground, it often wins. The largest wolves in the world are found in the moose country of Canada, Alaska and Russia, but it is a rare wolf that grows to more than 150 pounds (68 kg) in weight. Even here, most wolves are considerably lighter, weighing 80–100 pounds (36–45 kg). Scandinavian records show that super-wolves sometimes arise which acquire the skill to catch European elk unaided, but most Gray

The size of the wolf pack varies, but it is limited by the size of the prey which must be large enough to feed all the hunters.

75

wolves need the help of a pack of ten to twenty helpers. Many mouths make for more bites and quicker kills but many bellies must be filled as a consequence. The size of the pack is limited by the amount of meat on the prey. Wolf-packs that prey on white-tailed deer, which weigh only 154 pounds (70 kg), are necessarily smaller, with only seven to ten members.

There is not a wide variety of species of prey on the menu in Arctic and sub-Arctic habitats. This paucity is amply recompensed by the phenomenal numbers available. Juvenile Gray wolves often feed on rodents, even in areas where larger prey is abundant. Although they are virtually adult-sized, the yearlings like to hunt together in the summer, and they look for prey within their competence. In the north, during June and July, the ground is sometimes honeycombed by the tunnels of voles and lemmings. It is impossible to ignore the rodents, whose populations expand and contract in rhythmic cycles that correspond to the growth of the plants on which they feed. The first generations of a good rodent year are born early, beneath the snow. By late spring the burrows are seriously overcrowded and the ground squeaks piteously with each (human) footfall. As conditions underground deteriorate, generations of voles and lemmings are evicted to run the gauntlet of fox, owl and wolf. Adult wolves might not bother with such small fry – it won't feed the whole pack – but young wolves often bring rodents back to the den as a snack or plaything for the pups.

Territories vary enormously in size. Much depends on the climate and the quality of the grazing, for this determines the number of ungulates the land can support. In Superior National Forest, Minnesota, each pack claims 25–115 square miles (65–300 sq km) of exclusive territory. However, a study in Alaska showed a wolf-pack using an area of 5,000 square miles (8,000 sq km). Only birds claim larger terrestrial hunting grounds than wolves and their close relatives, wild dogs and hyenas.

It has been suggested that wolves have a beneficial effect on the populations of their prey. Certainly, wolves tend to remove the old and sickly from the herd, which leaves more grazing for vigorous males and females in the prime of life. The predation of wolves culls a number of young animals that probably would not survive the winter anyway. Where populations are closely monitored, it has been shown that, in some places, large numbers of ungulates die from starvation and disease during the winter months. The top predator in an ecosystem plays an important role in the health of that environment. It is argued that the presence of wolves, far from reducing the numbers of deer, may cause the population to rise, as culling improves the vitality of the breeding adults.

However, things are seldom as simple as that. Wolves do not choose their victims on the basis of what is good for the environment. They kill what they can get. Exceptionally harsh weather can set off a chain of events which may take years to work itself out. Cold winters are usually good for wolves, for as starvation saps the health of the deer, they become easier to catch. Later, in the spring, the calves are likely to be born underweight and susceptible to parasites and disease. In this situation both females and calves are more vulnerable to predation than usual, so the wolves eat well and, assisted by such a good start, more of their pups survive.

The following year the wolf-pack is larger than usual, so it needs more meat. The extra pressure may prevent the deer recovering their numbers so that

eventually the wolves themselves face starvation. The combination of shortage of food and lack of breeding opportunity forces the young wolves to peel away from their birth-pack. If they are successful in finding unoccupied countryside, the result could be a massive expansion in wolf territory and a substantial increase in the overall population. This is not the inevitable consequence of harsh winters, for many factors must be taken into account when calculating population dynamics, but the origins of the wolf's success as a species lie back in the Ice Age. A little cold has never hurt them.

Like bears, wolves sometimes vary their diet by catching fish as they make their spawning runs upriver. Not all wolves are fish-eaters, though. Fishing techniques are part of the hunting culture of certain packs, the skills passed on from one generation to another. Working from the rocks, wolves have been seen catching salmon by pawing them out of the water. Some trap jackfish or northern pike weighing up to 60 pounds (27 kg) by driving them into narrow channels of water. Adept wolves take advantage of the boggy areas that lie along the shores of lakes. They enter the larger channels in the network with a great deal of splashing, which frightens the fish into the shallows where they beach themselves. Some wolves fish for Arctic sculpin which they find by turning over

Young wolves are normally prevented from mating by the dominance of the alpha leader of their own sex. Frustration often causes them to leave the pack, striking out alone in the hope of finding a mate and new hunting territory.

Arctic wolves cooperate to hunt musk-oxen which form a defensive circle around their calves.

Below: Continually harrying the musk-oxen, the wolves try to break the circle and get their prey on the run.

rocks with their nose or paws, while slow-moving fish like suckers are easy to snatch directly from the water. Even shellfish sometimes appear in the wolf's diet. Until recently numerous wolves lived in the vast marshes of Southern Iraq where they probably subsisted entirely on a diet of fish and wild boar.

Wolves are often accused of unnecessary savagery. Of killing more than they need. Of taking pleasure in the slaughter, revelling in blood and death. Hunters, particularly those who want to justify torturing wolves themselves, quote the "evil nature" of wolves. Those sentences surely speak for themselves. However, overkill is a fact of life. Foxes do it when they get into a henhouse. Lions do it when they have the chance. Indeed, overkill may be a useful technique. Christina Dodwell reported from the Kamchatka Peninsula that although Siberian people dislike wolves, they credit them with great intelligence. They say that in winter wolf-packs actively try to drive reindeer into steep, narrow canyons. While half the pack pushes the deer forward, the other half separates to spring along the canyon ridge. Running in each other's tracks, the wolves' feet cut the snow to provoke an avalanche which collapses into the canyon and crushes the deer under tons of snow. This strategy is rather like putting meat in the deep freeze, for one kill can last the pack several months, perhaps all winter.

Wolves can eat up to 20 lb of meat at one meal, but they return to their kill to pick the bones for several days. Surplus meat is sometimes buried.

79

CHAPTER SEVEN

FRIENDS AND FOES

Surely it is obvious enough, if one looks at the whole world that it is
becoming daily better cultivated and more fully peopled. All places are
now accessible, all are well known; most pleasant farms have obliterated
all traces of what were once dreary and dangerous wastes; cultivated
fields and subdued forests, flocks and herds have expelled wild beasts;
sandy deserts are sown; rocks are planted; marshes are drained; and
where once were hardly solitary cottages, there are now large cities. No
longer are islands dreaded, nor their rocky shores feared; everywhere are
houses and inhabitants. Our teeming population is the strongest
evidence: our numbers are burdensome to the world which can hardly
supply us from its natural elements; our wants grow more and more
keen and our complaints more bitter in all mouths, whilst Nature fails in
affording us her usual sustenance. In every deed, pestilence, and famine
and wars, and earthquakes have to be regarded as a remedy for nations,
as the means of pruning the luxuriance of the human race.

Tertullian 337 A.D.

For nearly 2 million years the wolf ranged freely across the vast expanse of the Holarctic. It survived climatic change; it survived several transformations of the flora; it rode out ebbs and flows in the populations of the grazing animals on which it fed. The wolf is the quintessential survivor, one of the toughest, most adaptable and resilient mammals ever to walk the earth. Wolf and man are both intelligent, able to make certain deductions, but our imagination and our agriculture have transformed us from hunter–gatherers into beings that our ancestors would have instantly recognized as gods. Sadly, we are flawed masters. Having lost touch with the environment, we now imagine that we understand and control it. This illusion leads to deadly conflict.

Large predators are never short of enemies. Although wolves are responsible for only a small amount of predation on domestic stock – the figures are ridiculously low compared to damage caused by domestic dogs – the subject of their conservation has stirred the ire of a number of influential groups. For many rural people the psychological leap from the image of the wolf as incorrigible villain to that of respected member of a complete fauna is too large to make. Fortunately the wolf is accumulating a band of knowledgeable friends, and time (at last) may be on its side.

A new wave of environmental consciousness has swept the world. From

In the Cantabrian Mountains of Spain, where hunters have decimated wildlife for sport, wolves and farmers are forced to live in close proximity. As a result, wolves occasionally attack domestic stock.

Previous page: Although the world is not short of wilderness areas where wolves could be allowed to exist in natural conditions, hunters and farmers insist that strict control of numbers is necessary.

Antananarivo to Beijing, from Kamchatka to Chile, the word "conservation" is now understood by illiterate peasants as well as by the educated elite . Not everyone agrees with its interpretation, but most people have spared some time to think about the environment and how we should be functioning within it. As is to be expected, opinions vary. Two-thirds of the world's population are very poor and have no choice in how they scrape a living. They have frighteningly little capacity for sacrifice or change. Curiously, though, the main opponents to the establishment of environmental safeguards can be found in rich countries; the loggers of the American North-West, the whalers of Iceland, the fishermen and timber merchants of Japan and Korea. Corpulent vested interests speak loudest. When it comes to wolves, we find the strongest reactions voiced by organizations of cattle-ranchers, sports-hunters and property developers. None of these groups is in any way threatened by the existence of carefully monitored wolf-packs living, for the most part, in wilderness or sparsely populated areas. But the "devil wolf" is a powerful icon, capable of rousing extraordinary levels of fear and anxiety – and fear is a strong political weapon.

In North America and Europe the issue of wolf conservation has polarized into emotive campaigns and ruthless political maneuvering. On one side there is a growing body of largely urban preservationists, keen not only to protect the wolf in the habitats in which it survives today, but to reintroduce it to suitable National Parks and protected areas so that the wild fauna in these areas may be complete and have the opportunity to regulate itself in a natural way.

Hunters are wary of this view. They feel that any growth in wolf numbers will deplete what is left of wild ungulate stocks. In many parts of Europe and North

Far from avoiding humans, research shows that sometimes wolves live very close to man, quite unnoticed.

America, hunting for sport has seriously reduced populations of game animals such as deer and wild boar. Traditionally, the decline in game has always been blamed on the wolf, a convenient scapegoat that allows hunters to avoid the responsibility of self-control.

In many countries there is little left for hunters to shoot or for wolves to eat, so theoretically preservationists and hunters should have a lot in common. Both need to see the natural environment enhanced by careful management. Unfortunately, the popularity of hunting among a section of the population not noted for its sympathy towards authority has made cooperation difficult. The sheer escapism of hunting in North America is made all the more attractive by the strictures of city living. Associated with the pioneering spirit that built the country, hunting is seen as a cornerstone of the American Way of Life.

In Europe, peasants defend their unwritten "rights" to trap and shoot in spite of changes in national law created by agreements such as the Bern Convention of the Council of Europe (see Chapter 12). They know that few prosecutions will be brought. Witness the international scandal of the 6 million songbirds which are killed migrating across Europe each spring. European Community environment ministers wring their hands, but will not risk their political careers by enforcing the hunting laws. Like the bird migrants, wolves enjoy a measure of protection on paper, but in practice the law is not upheld.

When a law is passed in the United States, it is enforced by a government agency, the Department of Fish and Wildlife. When a law is passed in Europe, it seems that it may be completely ignored! The abyss that lies between conservation theory and practice is broad. This public hypocrisy not only denies the wolf the legal protection it is owed, but encourages hunters to believe they have some divine right to carry on shooting. It also encourages industrial and agricultural polluters, developers and other gross exploiters of the environment to believe themselves to be above the law.

In North America hunting is regarded as a business as much as a sport. A lot of people – hotel owners, restaurateurs, sports shop owners, guides and trackers, transport operators, gun manufacturers and salesmen – have a vested interest in keeping populations of game animals as high as possible. They demand that wolves should be strictly controlled, arguing that the economies of states which rely heavily on hunting are in jeopardy. Ranged with these businessmen stands a powerful beef and farming lobby. I myself have a lot of sympathy with farmers because I come from an agricultural family. Nevertheless, I have to express my astonishment at the way our planet is held to ransom by the cow! Of course, there are all kinds of farmers, rich and poor, some running operations more like factory conveyor belts, some using techniques which were old in Roman times. Although the former make the most noise, it is the latter who are usually at the sharp end of wolf conservation issues in countries like Spain, Greece, Iran, Italy and Russia.

Wolves do prey on domestic stock. There is no argument about that, yet the amount of damage they do is small. In the wolf country of northern Minnesota, it is estimated that there are around 7,000 farms, on which 296,000 cattle, up to 58,000 sheep and at least 682,000 turkeys were raised between 1975 and 1986. On average, only thirty farmers a year complained of wolf predation or sought compensation from the Minnesota Department of Agriculture, although there were at least 1,200 wolves in the state. In Minnesota, during the study period, they accounted for an average of only twenty-three cattle (mostly calves), forty-nine sheep and 173 turkeys. It seems that North American wolves generally keep clear of farms in spite of the fact that domestic stock are easy prey.

Although most farmers understand that wolves raid domestic stock because sheep and cattle have replaced the wild animals that were once freely available, the aftermath is always distressing. Although profit must be the bottom line in farming, many farmers do care for their animals, even though they are obviously not pets. Most are bound for market, but they are not quite commodities in the usual sense. Some farmers are actively involved in carefully planned breeding programmes and their animals are irreplaceable because they are the result of several generations of cross-breeding.

Dr Luigi Boitani has pointed out that traditional shepherds grazing their sheep in the mountains of Abruzzi, Italy, have developed certain practices to guard against the wolves. They bring their sheep off the high slopes at dusk and pen them in corals where they can be watched. They know that wolves are active during the day as well as at night if the weather is cloudy, so they are extra vigilant during bad weather. These shepherds do not hate wolves, they have learned to live with them and to minimize damage. For centuries sheep have shared the mountains with wolves, but now attitudes are changing. Modern shepherds do not want to watch their flocks at night, they want to stay at home and watch television like everyone else. As a result, in many areas flocks are much larger and more vulnerable than they used to be. Visiting shepherds, who bring their sheep to the mountain pastures in summer, are not always familiar with local practices and on a few occasions wolves have killed large numbers of animals. This strains the relationship with the farming community, reinforcing the false image of the wolf as an evil monster, killing for pleasure.

It is the wasteful nature of the overkill which farmers find particularly distressing. They can accept – albeit grudgingly – occasional predation, but react in understandable horror to the sight of an entire flock butchered. Biologist, Paul

Leyhausen describes hunting as a series of episodes: stalking, running, killing and eating. Each phase of the hunt has its own objectives which must be satisfied before the next phase in the sequence is triggered off. The stimuli which cause a wolf to run, to kill and to eat are irresistible. When cattle or sheep react in panic, they are firing "kill" stimuli at the wolf which it cannot ignore. It is behavior born of an unnatural situation. In the wild, wolves only kill to satisfy their needs. They do not kill for entertainment.

Small farmers simply cannot afford to lose a proportion of their stock to wolves. It is the profit margin on which they depend. A self-employed farmer is dependent on the vagaries of weather and markets for his income, which is often modest. Farmers attempting to wrest a living from marginal lands at the edge of wild habitats cannot support wolves, so everyone concerned with conservation is agreed that farmers who suffer damage from wolf predation should be adequately compensated. Unfortunately, there are many problems associated with making such payments. Is the actual value of the animal taken into account? Or the price it would have fetched at market? After all, the farmer has lost not only the beast, but its potential, which presumably he was counting on to make his own living. The trouble is that authorities cannot pay more than the animal was worth at the time of its death without encouraging wholesale abuse of the compensation system. Who, then, is to fix the sum? All around the world, it is obvious that while compensation must be paid if wolves are to be protected, there are procedural problems.

Perhaps the most sorely felt dissatisfaction from the farmers' point of view is the difficulty in getting their hands on the money. Payments have been delayed for months or even years in Italy, Spain and Portugal. In some countries payments are only made if the wolves strayed from public lands, such as National Parks. If the wolves have come from private estates, the farmer who has suffered the loss is expected to sue the landowner himself. Satisfaction is rare.

One further complication to the compensation issue is the tendency for a few dishonest farmers to exaggerate the damage by making fraudulent claims. This is less common nowadays, however, as officials charged with monitoring compensation payments have acquired the experience to judge the cause of death.

Wolf damage is complicated in Europe and Asia by the existence of a massive population of unsupervised domestic as well as feral dogs. Research has shown that dogs do far more damage than wolves, but it is generally wolves that get the blame. Curiously, in Italy it is not the feral dogs that kill the most stock, but gangs of domestic dogs on the rampage. After the carnage they return to their various homes, wagging their tails. The owner, seeing his pooch assuming its customary subservience, cannot believe the animal has had any part in the slaughter. In Great Britain (where there are no wolves to blame) farmers are familiar with the behavior of pet dogs and shoot them if they are seen worrying sheep. In Spain farmers must hold their fire, for the hunting lobby is powerful. Hunters often use several dogs for the chase. They frequently get lost and are often abandoned by their masters who give up searching for them as dusk falls. This has created a major feral dog problem in remote areas where the dogs must kill or starve.

Whatever the real cause of death, the story often finds its way to the local newspaper and strict accuracy is seldom allowed to interfere with recounting a good tale. Newspaper owners have, after all, yet to be sued for libel by a pack of wolves. Fierce animal stories are good copy splashed all over the front page to feed the thrill of old fears. Archives show this to be a timeworn practice, going back generations of editors to the very birth of publishing.

The biologist and film-maker, Erik Zimen carried out a small survey on public awareness in the Abruzzi.

> The farther we were from the areas in which wolves lived, the more dangerous they were believed to be. In areas inhabited by wolves, those least impressed by their alleged dangerousness were those who had direct contact with them. The occupational group that regarded the wolf as especially dangerous was, interestingly enough, innkeepers.

So the wolf has many enemies. A few of these are devious, using the wolf's bad reputation for their own ends, but the majority are simply misinformed. If wolves are not to be driven to extinction by mindless hatred, fact must be sifted from fiction. A phenomenal amount of scientific work has accumulated over the last forty years, and this is now being used effectively by conservation societies devoted to straightening the record. The International Wolf Centre in Minnesota, inspired by leading wolf biologist L. David Mech, prints a quarterly magazine, *International Wolf*, with contributions from a variety of wolf writers. Things are moving ahead in Minnesota where the 1990 state legislature appropriated 1.2 million dollars for the support of the Centre, and the Science Museum of Minnesota has granted a 6,000-square-foot (2,000-sq-m) 'Wolves and Humans' exhibit for permanent display. The North American Wildlife Park Foundation publishes an equally thorough magazine called *Wolf!*, under the guidance of wolf behaviorist Erich Klinghammer.

Although in Europe communication is complicated by the existence of several major languages, the Portuguese Grupo Lobo (see also Chapter 12) triumphs with a low-budget newsletter which cuts through the cant of hunters and politicians, delivering scientific news about wolves from Mongolia to Mexico, together with an appraisal of the various sociological and legal issues associated with their conservation. Led by Robert Lisle, Grupo Lobo's work with both wild and captive wolves has so effectively reeducated the people of Portugal that the wolf was voted "Favorite Animal of the Year" in a popular survey in 1992.

Information is the prime weapon of all conservation groups which seek to change public consciousness. Although no one would pretend that it is an easy matter to protect wolves, statistics may help to lay to rest our fear of them. No wolves – or coyotes – are mentioned in the following bulletin from *The Animals' Agenda*, May 1992.

> Last year, in Assam (India), thirty-one people were killed by elephants. . . . In the USA some 200 individuals were killed by or died through the agency of animals (hunting and traffic accidents, etc.) . . . specifically, in order of the number of deaths caused, by white-tailed deer, bees, dogs, wild turkeys (eight hunters killed each other while trying to kill turkeys), rattlesnakes, spiders, sharks, captive elephants, scorpions, rats, goats, captive leopards, jelly fish, coral snakes, alligators, grizzly bears, mountain lions, captive monkeys, vultures and orcas. (Quoted by Grupo Lobo *Newsletter*, Vol. 7, No. 3, 1992.)

Above: A radio-collar enables scientists to trace a wolf's movements and hunting activities over a period of several months.

Wolverine and wolfskins are used to make a warm parka hood in the traditional style of north American native people.

CHAPTER EIGHT

A SPACE FOR THE WOLF IN THE UNITED STATES

Of all the native biological constituents of a northern wilderness scene, I should say that wolves present the greatest test of human wisdom and good intentions.

Paul L. Errington, *Of Predation and Life* (University of Iowa Press, 1967)

The great difference between the wolves of North America and those of Europe lies in their long-term relationship with man. The wolf-packs of Europe have existed at the edge of human civilization for well over 2,000 years. By comparison, the American wolf was always an animal of the wilderness — essentially the wild creature of a pristine habitat – until well into the nineteenth century.

When the first wagons rolled west across the North American plains, the pioneers found, to their astonishment, a land grazed by literally millions of bison. The frontier was not empty but already inhabited by numerous native Americans. As though this were not enough, they discovered their vision of a prosperous future infested by wolves. Bison, Indians and wolves were all three in the way of agricultural progress as defined by wave upon wave of settlers from every corner of the Old World, who arrived with an urgent need to find land and make a living. The elimination of the bison was a priority, for the grazing was required by the cow. As the great beasts were slaughtered by the hundred thousand, shot by professional hunters, ranchers and sportsmen in an orgy of blood and newly forged patriotic zeal, wolves padded out of the wilderness to howl around the camps of the killers — normal behavior for a scavenger. Although at first the wolves doubtless prospered, gorging on the unwanted bison corpses left to rot on the plain, their days were numbered. Settlers grew tired of their presence and organized massive wolf hunts along European lines, involving every gun-totin' man in the area in what was almost a "holy war."

Neither could the Indians be permitted to flourish. They watched the physical destruction of their environment with anger and despair; saw the end of their own frugal hunting, the erosion of their culture and the theft of their freedom. Wolves and Indians. Varmints and outcasts in their own land.

At first the white men's cattle roamed free, but soon thousands of miles of barbed wire were required to protect the Hereford stock, imported from Europe at great expense in order to improve the blood-lines of America's holy cow.

89

Now protected by the Endangered Species Act, wolves in the lower forty-eight states of the USA have a chance of recovery. Already, wolves are returning to areas from which they were once extirpated.

Previous page: Wolves remain numerous in Canada and Alaska where relatively enlightened management has prevented the sort of slaughter that virtually eliminated the wolf from the lower forty-eight states of the USA.

Wolves were perceived as a particular danger to confined stock, so in most states a system of bounties was introduced. A dead wolf was worth 3 dollars in Minnesota in 1849. The aim was nothing short of extermination, and across most of the lower forty-eight states of the United States that is exactly what was achieved. Guns and traps were employed everywhere, but it was poison – mostly strychnine – that finally extirpated the wolf from virtually its entire traditional range. It was a long and bitter struggle, and it is a tribute to the intelligence of the wolf and the effectiveness of its breeding strategy that many populations held on until well into the twentieth century. After 100 years of killing, bounties were still being offered for wolves during the 1950s.

The Endangered Species Act of 1967 was the start of a complete change in the official attitude to the wolf in the United States. The first Endangered Species Act simply listed the wolf and offered no protection, but a second Act in 1973 legislated to protect the wolf from being killed anywhere in the forty-eight contiguous states. Outraged ranchers and hunters simply could not understand the change of heart, asking, "Why protect wolves when we bountied them only ten years ago?" Tempers flared at rowdy public meetings and dead wolves were

The Mexican wolf Canis lupus baileyi *is the smallest subspecies of wolf in North America. Less than 50 survive in the Mexican states of Chihuahua and Durango.*

dumped on the steps of government buildings in protest against the new law. Ranchers pointed out that while the wolf was arguably endangered in the lower forty-eight states, it was common enough over the border in Canada, and that Alaska boasted so many wolves that a vigorous control programme was in operation. In spite of these inconsistencies, the official line gradually prevailed. Recovery plans were drawn up to allow wolves to recolonize suitable areas. There was a new sense that wolves had an important role to play in nature, and that we should try to discover what it might be. Underlying the scientific argument in favour of biodiversity was the feeling that we needed to atone for the mindless slaughter of earlier years.

The United States Fish and Wildlife Service made plans to restore the wolf, creating an Eastern Timber Wolf Recovery Team to deal with areas east of the Great Plains, with a second Recovery Team to plan a strategy for the Rocky Mountains. Each team was made up of a mix of wolf experts and representatives of land management agencies.

The wolves of Minnesota had a head-start. It was the only member of the lower forty-eight states in which a healthy breeding population had survived. As poaching decreased, Minnesota's wolves flourished, monitored by an enthusiastic band of scientists and well-wishers. By the mid-1970s the wolves were colonizing areas they had not been seen in for twenty years and were even dispersing into nearby Wisconsin and Michigan. Fresh blood came to Minnesota with immigrant wolves from Ontario, Canada. In spring 1993 the population is optimistically thought to run to 1,750 animals, while the population of neighboring Wisconsin is estimated to be about forty and Michigan about thirty (including Isle Royale). Further west, separated from Minnesota by the states of North and South Dakota, Montana has a breeding population of about forty wolves. The wolf is classed as a threatened animal in Minnesota, but it is listed as an endangered species in the other states, a category that ensures its protection. There is considerable demand from hunters and ranchers for the wolf to be removed from the endangered list, but this will not happen until the population has risen to at least 100 wolves in areas which can be replenished from the Minnesota population, or at least 200 animals in areas that are more than 100 miles (160 km) from Minnesota. The new populations will have to prove their viability over a period of five years. The Wisconsin wolf will be reclassified as "threatened" when the late winter census records eighty wolves for three consecutive years.

In spite of threats from diseases such as heartworm, Lyme disease and canine parvo virus (a new disease of dogs), the Minnesota recovery seems unstoppable. Thirteen wolf-packs were monitored during the winter of 1992–3 and it was calculated that the population had increased by 35 percent since the previous year. Currently there is one wolf for every 12 square miles (20 sq km) of suitable territory. Writing in the month of March, I think of the yearling wolves who are at this very moment dispersing across the frigid landscape. Where the first pioneer treads, others will follow, through the woods and across the hills in search of mates and fresh hunting grounds. Studies of white-tailed deer indicate a ratio of 200 deer to every wolf in the state. Minnesota's wolves will travel on a full belly.

The fate of the wolves of Lake Superior's Isle Royale does not seem so hopeful. When the first two wolves wandered across the ice to the island during the

After years of political wrangling over whether wolves should be reintroduced to Yellowstone National Park, wild pioneers are moving south down the Rocky Mountains, to recolonize the area naturally.

Professional wolfers like Dick Brown, pictured at his camp near Fallon, Montana, were responsible for exterminating the wolf from most of the USA. A pile of leghold traps lying by the tent is testimony to his method.

particularly cold winter of 1949, they became the subjects of one of the world's longest-running ecological studies. For the last thirty-four years the wolves have been monitored in an attempt to discover the mechanisms behind their population dynamics. Unable to leave the 210-square-mile (338-sq-km) island, the wolves have been dependent on the resident herd of moose (European elk) for winter food. At first their population rose and fell with that of the moose, but after a few years this relationship changed.

It was thought that the wolf and moose populations would fluctuate in a cyclical manner, both regulating themselves in a sustainable way. If the wolves killed too many moose, although they would raise extra pups the first year, they would go hungry later. If the enlarged pack seriously overexploited the moose, most would ultimately starve. It was calculated that there would always be a few

moose and a few wolves left to make a recovery and that eventually some kind of balance would be struck.

Reality has proved more complicated. At one point wolf numbers climbed to a record fifty animals (one wolf for every 4 square miles (6 sq km) of territory) but the population unexpectedly crashed between 1980 and 1982. It has never recovered, and today the pack numbers only twelve animals. This is strange because there are currently 1,600 moose on Isle Royale – more than anyone can remember. Numerous underweight and sickly calves can be seen, which is a clear sign that the moose are overexploiting the habitat. Many of these moose are old and tick-infested. Normally they would be extremely vulnerable, but the wolf-pack seems unable to take advantage of the situation. Clearly factors other than the predator–prey relationship are at work.

Cut off from the mainland, the wolves of Isle Royale are heavily inbred, with many genetic characteristics which indicate that the cause of their decline could be inbreeding depression. Genetic fingerprinting shows that the surviving wolves are as closely related as siblings. The survivors do not seem physically odd, but the population is producing only three pups each year, which is not enough for them to regain their old numbers. Wolves are essentially travelers, and dispersal is an important part of their breeding strategy. On Isle Royale, the younger

United States' Forest Service hunters display their finest pelts.

wolves cannot disperse to found new packs, and no fresh blood infiltrates the established families. The consequences may prove fatal for the entire population. Scientists have agreed a policy of non-interference in the dynamics of the pack, so they can only wait to see what the future holds.

Far to the west of the Minnesota crucible, in Washington State, wolves are sometimes seen in the Glacier Peaks Wilderness and the Lake Chelan area, Okanagan National Forest and the Ross Lake National Recreation area. People are encouraged to report sightings by ringing a toll-free telephone number (1–800–722–4095). No recovery plan exists for these areas, but the Northern Rocky Mountain Wolf Recovery Plan could be coordinated to encompass the entire north-west United States.

There is certainly plenty of suitable wolf habitat in the roadless wilderness of Central Idaho, where there may be six to eight wolves. One of these individuals was radio-collared in Glacier National Park before being tracked to Idaho's Clearwater National Forest in late January 1992. Although the public is understandably cautious about the presence of wolves, over 70 percent of Idaho's citizens were in favour of their presence in suitable areas.

The recovery of wolves in the United States is a delicate business. As Dr L. David Mech has pointed out, the Endangered Species Act has been "a howling success," but behind the overall increase in wolf numbers lies a situation which could backfire on the preservationists, rather in the way that on the west coast an endangered bird, the Spotted owl, has polarized loggers and conservationists into two belligerent groups, implacably opposed to each other.

The battle over the future of North America's last temperate rainforests – the old-growth forests of the North-West – has roused bitter emotions. The Japanese, who are conserving what's left of their own pristine forest, are prepared to pay seven times the value of ordinary timber for the towering cedar and spruce of North America. Under United States law there is no way the timber industry can be restrained from clear-felling the ancient forests of the west coast except by invoking the protection of a rare species – the Spotted owl.

Farmers opposed to reintroduction of wolves view the Endangered Species Act with deep suspicion. They have seen the fights and lawsuits surrounding the owl. Now they are nervous of government interference and control. They are concerned that the presence of an endangered animal on their land – the wolf, this time – might lead to restrictions on their agricultural activities. The last thing they want to do is manage the land for wildlife!

Yet in what plight would endangered animals find themselves without the Act? In 1980 the Red wolf, which until recently was regarded as a separate species, became extinct in the wild in the United States. Throughout the 1960s it was obvious that hybridization with coyotes would wipe out the last of these interesting wolves, but nothing could be done except to capture specimens. When the Endangered Species Act was passed in 1973, the United States Department of Fish and Wildlife was at last empowered to take action, and a recovery program was started. Based on breeding genetically pure Red wolves in captivity, the idea was to return them to suitable habitats where they could establish themselves free of persecution. It was to be the first attempt anywhere in the world to reintroduce a carnivore back into an area from where it had been extirpated. Recognizing the importance of the project, the recovery program involved the cooperation of twenty-five zoos and an annual budget that increased from 30,000 dollars to 191,000 dollars in 1992.

By 1976 a founder population of seventeen Red wolves was established, and the following year the first pups were born at the Point Defiance Zoological Gardens in Tacoma, Washington. By 1988 there were eighty Red wolves in captivity in eight locations around the United States. The public required a good deal of persuasion, but following an education program designed to allay fears, the first ten individuals were released into Alligator River National Wildlife Refuge in North Carolina in 1987. They were carefully monitored, and in time twenty-six more animals were introduced. Some had to be recaptured, some died, but today six of the original group are still free-ranging and they have begun to breed. Agreements made with adjacent landowners allow the new Red wolf population legally to inhabit about 367 square miles (95,000 hectares) of federal and private land in eastern North Carolina. The wolf conservationists hope that between fifty and 100 wolves will be restored over the next ten years.

Preservationists have been able to lobby for special treatment and funding to support the Red wolf project because of its status as a separate species, highly endangered and therefore absolutely protected by law. However, new genetic evidence suggests that the Red wolf has acquired coyote genes somewhere along the path of its evolution. In the light of this information, taxonomists may reclassify the animal, and this could affect the financial budget devoted to its reintroduction.

Gray wolves and coyotes can interbreed (as can wolves and dogs) and their offspring are fertile. This capacity points to a very close relationship between all three species. Interbreeding has probably occurred many times over the last few million years in response to natural phenomena like climatic change. Now it seems that Red wolves, Mexican wolves and those found in Eurasia too, are using the same survival tool to adapt to man-made changes in the environment. Scientific controversy is bound to rage for some time to come, but at the moment many believe that the Red wolf is probably best described as a subspecies of the Gray wolf.

No one really knows whether the Mexican wolf (another subspecies of the Gray wolf) is extinct in the wild or not. At the moment there are forty-two adults in captivity, spread around nine institutions in the Unites States and ten in Mexico. An Environmental Impact Statement is being prepared and it is possible that reintroductions could be made to suitable habitats in Arizona following an educational program and public consultation.

A battle has arisen over the issue of returning the Rocky Mountain wolf to Yellowstone National Park, where preservationists are demanding the conservation of a full complement of flora and fauna in obedience to the original mandate of the National Parks Service. The wolf was extirpated from the Park in 1926 in spite of the fact that it was set up specifically to preserve complete natural systems. The pro-wolf lobby points out that the wolves are unlikely to seriously diminish the American elk (*Cervus canadensis*) population. Quite the opposite, their presence will improve the health of the herd by culling the old and the weak, which will allow breeding animals in their prime to enjoy better grazing. Many deer starve to death every winter in Yellowstone National Park, so the reintroduction of wolves will allow a different – perhaps more natural – regulation of numbers. The park encompasses some 3,472 square miles (8,888 sq km) of land which carries 20–30,000 elk, *Cervus canadensis* (these are not

One of the original Nine Mile Valley pups about to be translocated. The litter was protected after the parents were killed and their movements were monitored by means of radio-collars. Their existence in Montana stirred up a storm of publicity. To begin with the pups thrived on wild prey but most of the litter was translocated by officials after two steers were attacked.

Montana hunters are alerted to the presence of wolves in the area and tactfully reminded that they are a protected species.

European elk, or moose, but deer known as wapiti in Asia), around 3,000 mule deer and 2,700 bison, together with smaller numbers of moose (European elk), pronghorn, bighorn and mountain goats.

The situation would seem ideal, but the anti-wolf lobby argues that the land around the Park is unsuitable for reintroduction. Long narrow valleys along the Park borders would funnel wolves, game, livestock and people together in densities which, it is claimed, will cause excessive predation and damage to domestic stock. This area of the Rockies is physically different to the plains of Minnesota, and no one would pretend that wolves can be contained within the Park boundaries. Local people are contemptuous of the films shown by some conservation groups that portray the wolf "too sympathetically." Ranchers remember that the last wolves were forced out of these mountains in the 1930s only after a long struggle. They do not see why they should put the clock back.

The matter of wolves for Yellowstone has been under discussion since 1970. Long held up by political maneuvering, an Environmental Impact Study – a prerequisite to reintroduction – has at last been completed. The study's investigations have included an eduction program and a series of public meetings in major cities to "scope" the opinions of citizens. Although rural dwellers have remained cautious, the overwhelming consensus of opinion is that the wolf should be reintroduced to Yellowstone. For the majority of Americans the wolf is no longer an object of fear, but a symbol of people's new commitment to nature. In spite of the difficulties – and the cost – they want the wolf.

It is probably true that when the wolf returns to Yellowstone it will be there for ever. It seems likely that this stronghold will, year after year, send out dispersing wolves, some of whom will doubtless try to colonize areas outside the boundary of the Park. It is a fact of life that preservationists must accept that many of these wolves will die. As the population climbs, official control measures will undoubtedly be needed to protect farmers' stock. Within the Park the wolves will be unmolested, but because they are an artificially introduced population they may not enjoy complete legal protection outside its boundaries. Under the Endangered Species Act they will be designated an "experimental/non-essential population." As such they will probably be "subject to management by state wildlife officials." They will almost certainly be shot.

After years of delay, a decision was made in Spring 1993 to proceed at once with an official reintroduction programme. The project was almost redundant, for wild Canadian wolves were already crossing the border, threading their way south over the passes and down through the valleys of the Rocky Mountains. The first immigrant arrived in Glacier National Park, Montana during 1987. Others have followed and some have given birth to litters, among them the famous Nine Mile Pack, born in the Nine Mile Valley, Montana.

Orphaned early in life, the Nine Mile wolves did not have the opportunity to learn from their parents how to catch wild prey. To survive they attacked two steers and, as a result, all but one were rounded up and relocated. To the delight of many, two new wolves have appeared in the valley, giving birth to pups in 1992. The Nine Mile Pack lives!

Inside Yellowstone Park there have already been a few sightings of wild wolves, and they are seen increasingly in the mountains and forests between Cody and the Montana border. It is certain that the pioneers will eventually find the right place to settle down. This will not be an "experimental" group but a truly wild population of wolves.

Although the anti-wolf lobby started out with plenty of ammunition to thwart the dreams of America's preservationists, they have been largely disarmed by a careful education program led by Yellowstone Campaign organizer Renee Askins. The idea of reintroducing the wolf to its traditional habitats was born over twenty years ago, but it has taken time to gather and present enough scientific evidence to refute the fears of ranchers. Years of patient work are coming to fruition as attitudes change. The work of American wolf preservationists is also showing the way to naturalists in Europe who are struggling to protect ever-shrinking populations of wolves against those old enemies, fear and prejudice.

CHAPTER NINE

THE QUESTION OF CONTROL

*If we knock half of a wolf population out every year, we may soon end
up with the same number of wolves again, because they can breed
rapidly, but we've basically shredded this underlying social fabric, which
so sets them apart.*

Dr. Gordon Haber, from an interview in Wolves and Related Canids
Newsletter Summer 1992

A seemingly innocent raffle in British Columbia in 1984 was the start of an
international furore over the vexed matter of wolf management. The
government of the United States of America has spent millions of dollars on
programs to protect and reintroduce wolves in the lower forty-eight contiguous
states, but in Alaska wolves are far from being an endangered species. They are
also common in Canada, where they have always been hunted by native
Americans for their outstandingly warm fur. The arrival of European trappers,
traders and farmers changed the nature of this hunting. Wolves were no longer
occasionally killed to provide for local needs, but "harvested" to supply distant
markets for cash. Although attitudes to the wolf have altered in the United States,
trapping and shooting are still officially encouraged north of the border where it
is feared that wolves may "get out of hand." This attitude is found in all countries
where wolves are numerous.

The business of wolf-killing raises many questions. First of all, is it really
necessary? And if, in certain circumstances, wolves must be killed, how many
shall die and what impact will that have on the environment? Who shall kill
them, and by what method? Who will determine the death-roll? While hunters
regard wolves and their prey as a resource, millions of nature lovers are voicing a
quite different philosophy.

Until recently the state of Alaska, as well as Canada and Russia, managed its
wolves from the point of view of maintaining good stocks of game animals and
protecting cattle, sheep and domestic reindeer. Nobody questioned these policies
too much; after all, the population of wolves seemed vigorous, what did it
matter?

However, when the British Columbian Wildlife Federation sponsored a raffle
to fund a wolf-shooting jamboree by helicopter in 1984, they stirred up a
hornets' nest of publicity. Amazed animal lovers learned that first prize for the

lucky winner was to be an African hunting safari. A whole body of opinion that had never before been heard started to inundate newspapers and television stations with radically different views on the subject of wolves. People who saw the wolf as a symbol of wilderness and freedom were incensed by the thoughtless destruction of such a magnificent wild predator. The idea that some raffle-winner might travel to Africa to kill more magnificent wild predators over there, was deeply abhorrent.

The resulting uproar caused a reappraisal of the killing policy, not only in Canada but in Alaska too. It has taken some time to convince provincial legislature, but slowly – after nine years – a new consciousness is arising. People are questioning the old assumptions and asking wolf managers, politicians, scientists and conservationists to reevaluate what wolves really mean to us. Last year tourists visiting National Parks in the Canadian Yukon were asked to name their favourite animal, the species they would most like to see. The reply was "The Wolf." The once-feared predator has been transformed into the most popular attraction of the year!

The opinion of conservationists and animal lovers no longer reflects a minority view. Yukon managers calculate that the "non-consumptive use" of wildlife by tourists exceeds its consumptive use by hunters and trappers thirty times over. It is a new way of looking at an old problem, but has it led to any change?

As a result of comparatively enlightened policies it is estimated that over 50,000 wolves live on Canadian soil today. Each province has its own regulations for wolf control, which vary with local conditions. In the Yukon, the wolf population has recently risen from 5,900 to around 7,200. This increase is not the result of "going soft" on wolves. Aircraft are still used for hunting and trapping in spite of the shift in public attitudes.

In British Columbia, where the controversy started, wolf working groups were set up to give the public a chance to comment on wolf management in the province. The idea was to incorporate the concerns of all sections of the community in forming provincial strategy. Sadly, opinions were too polarized. Some people wanted all the wolves protected, while hunters in the north complained that all the game was gone and insisted on the need for wolf control. No one could agree on anything, and the meetings faltered. British Columbia has not yet found a compromise or published a management plan.

The province of Alberta has 27,280 square miles (440,000 sq km) of suitable wild wolf habitat within its borders. The northern half of the province together with the mountainous area bordering British Columbia are sparsely settled by man, and wolves exist in near natural densities. Here, according to a recent state management plan, they are "valued inhabitants of natural ecosystems . . . that should be maintained at a winter population of 4,000 in the long term."

The province of Alberta already has 4,000 wolves, so it doesn't want any more. To hold the population down, wolf "control" has become a regular part of habitat management. A healthy wolf population breeds so freely that in Alberta it has been calculated that 20–25 percent of the wolves must be culled if the population is to stay the same.

So each year about 300 trappers are trained in the techniques of wolf-killing and are provided with free snares to start them off. In some places, where state scientists believe that the wolf population is seriously out of balance with its prey, or where wolves are being "troublesome," a bounty might be offered or

Previous page: Magnificent symbol of wilderness and freedom? Or nothing but a predatory varmint? Americans holding radically different views on wildlife are confronting each other over the future of the wolf.

104

contract trappers sent in to make the kills. Around 50,000 dollars a year are paid out in compensation for the loss of cattle or sheep to wolves, so private citizens are encouraged to shoot and trap them whenever they can. No license is required. There is a long hunting season from early September to the end of May but this does not affect landowners or leaseholders who can kill wolves on their own property at any time. It remains legal to use baits and electronic calling devices to lure the wolves within range and there is no limit on the number of wolves a resident Albertan can kill. Poisoning is illegal because it is almost impossible to ensure that wolves alone take the bait. Countless other animals die, not just the individuals who take the bait directly but hundreds more who become affected as the poison makes its way into the food chain. Nevertheless, Compound 1080, which is more lethal to canids than to other animals, is often used by government officers who are called out to kill an average of sixty-seven wolves a year.

It all seems very sad, not to say incongruous, when one thinks of the efforts to protect the species being made just over the border in the United States. Alberta's own management report acknowledges that "many wolves living near livestock do not prey on them." The trouble is, as farmers are quick to point out, that it is

Shocked and distressed, its fur standing on end in fear, a wolf is caught by both forefeet in a double leghold trap. It may have been suffering for several days.

hard to distinguish marauding wolves from innocent bystanders. In the predominantly agricultural south of the province, wolves are shot on sight. At present it is only in National Parks like Banff and Jasper that they enjoy full protection.

Canada's system of National Parks is currently being extended. Since Banff was created in 1885 only 1.8 percent of Canada has been preserved in National Parks. Now the federal government is committed to establish at least five new terrestrial parks by 1996 and to sign agreements on thirteen more by the year 2000. This Green Plan will preserve about 3 percent of Canada, going some way towards the 12 percent recommended by the Brundtland Commission.

Unfortunately, when it comes to management, wolves feature rather low on the list of priorities. Wood Buffalo National Park is famous for its Black wolves. The biggest canids in the world, they feed on bison, the American continent's largest prey. In Wood Buffalo National Park, there are up to 200 wolves following 3,500 bison, and a pack of ten kills an adult bison (or the equivalent)

Removing wolf pups from the den.

Opposite: In Canada wolves are only protected inside National Parks.

The wolves in Wood Buffalo National Park, Canada, are threatened by the proposed slaughter of their prey, the Park's bison, in an attempt to eradicate bovine brucellosis and tuberculosis from the herd.

about once a week. The park boasts one of the highest densities of wolves in the world, concentrated in the Peace Athabasca delta where there is one wolf every 1.6 square miles (2.6 sq km).

The Park was originally established in 1922 to protect the Wood bison subspecies, but between 1925 and 1928 over 6,000 Plains bison were brought in from Wainwright, Alberta. Many of them were infected with bovine brucellosis and tuberculosis, which have been active in the hybrid population ever since. Agriculture Canada (the national Department of Agriculture) is pressing for the slaughter of the entire bison herd at Wood Buffalo National Park in accordance with its policy to eliminate these diseases from all animals, both domestic and wild, throughout Canada. The idea is to replace the diseased hybrids with pure Wood bison stock, untainted by disease. But this could not be done overnight. During the changeover, many wolves would die as their prey were removed. Another problem lies in taxonomy of the bison. Recent studies suggest that there are no grounds at all for preserving the Wood bison as a separate subspecies; genetically they are all Plains bison.

Conservationists accuse agricultural and industrial interests of "conspiracy," pointing out that recent reductions in the bison population are not caused by disease but by major flooding in the late 1960s and the drying-out of the delta by the Bennett hydroelectric dam built upstream on the Peace River. They say commercial interests are dictating the future of the park which, far from being a protected haven for wildlife, is permitting serious commercial exploitation within its boundaries, which includes the logging of old-growth trees by a Japanese company.

An equally fierce controversy over the future of wolves is raging in Alaska, where angry hunters accuse animal-loving conservationists of using the wolf issue in an attempt to ban all hunting. Alaska, traditionally a "frontier" state in every sense, has a healthy population of between 5,900 and 7,900 wolves, in spite of the fact that they have been routinely shot, trapped and poisoned for well over a century. During the last decade an average of 842 wolves (11–14 percent) have been killed each year, often by people using aircraft for "land-and-shoot" hunting, nevertheless Alaska provably supports more wolves now than at anytime since achieving Statehood in 1959.

Aerial hunting is hardly sporting, but there are few roads into the wilderness. Aircraft are often the only means of access to many areas, where the wolves are located from the plane before landing to conduct the hunt. "Land-and-shoot" hunting is allowed only in specific areas where a wolf-control program has been authorized. Alaska Department of Fish and Game officers claim to enforce the regulations rigorously. The misuse of aircraft for hunting in Alaska attracts a 5,000-dollar fine and a maximum of six months in jail.

A great deal of effort has been made to determine the complex relationship between predator and prey, with a view to judging the value of "wolf control." Human hunters cannot be left out of the equation and both Black and Grizzly bears are also predators of caribou and moose (European elk). Wildlife managers are reluctant to shoot bears because they have a slow rate of reproduction and would take many years to recover. Wolves, on the other hand, bounce back. The figures prove it.

Many Alaskans depend on moose and caribou for food, so wolf control is a hot issue in traditional rural communities where hunters are convinced that more wolves mean less game. Supplies of domestic meat are imported from the south because ranching is impossible in Alaska. Raised on agricultural feeds, fattened through the use of hormone injections, protected by antibiotics and other drugs; this beef is inferior to game, say the hunters, who suggest that culling wild deer is a much more environmentally friendly way of obtaining meat. They have a point. It is estimated that it costs ten calories of energy in foodstuffs to produce one calorie of beef. Wild animals, on the other hand, thrive on wilderness plants which provide "free" energy.

Aware of the deep divisions in the community, the Alaska Board of Game, which is charged with the control of wolves over an area twice the size of Texas, consulted a cross-section of citizens at a series of public mdeetings. In 1992 it proposed a draft management plan designed to maintain the wolf population at just below its natural level in some areas, but to severely curtail wolf numbers in 3.5 percent of the State where moose and caribou stocks were falling. Full protection for wolves was to be extended from 2 percent to 3 percent of the State. A map was proposed, describing six areas for different intensities of wolf management. Although carefully drawn up in association with wolf experts and preservationists as well as hunters, the Alaska Wolf Management Plan pleased no-one. The Alaska Wildlife Alliance – while insisting that it did not oppose

Brought to the brink of extinction by buffalo hunters in the nineteenth century, Plains bison are slowly recovering their numbers inside the protection of national parks. In Canada, their population is controlled naturally by wolves.

traditional hunting – pronounced its members unhappy with zoning. Together with the Northern Alaska Center for the Environment, the Anchorage Chapter of the National Audubon Society, Greenpeace, the National Parks and Conservation Association, and Fund for Animals, they demanded more protection for wolves.

Accompanied by a fanfare of misleading tabloid publicity, a media-war in public relations broke out. While hunters demanded that aerial-hunting be relegalized as a sport, preservationists announced that Alaska intended to "destroy" its "vulnerable" wolf population by means of a massive air-strike, and took out advertising space to rally some 40,000 people from the lower 48 states to write or telephone Alaska's governor, Walter J. Hickel, threatening to cancel their vacations. When forecasts indicated a loss to the state in the region of 85 million dollars, the Governor called a meeting at Fairbanks in January 1993.

Everyone was there: well-known wolf experts, grizzled hunters, eager preservationists and animal welfare activists. They were divided into nine working groups to discuss (once again) the issues involved. At the end of two days they did not manage to reach consensus, but they did agree that wolf control could be considered under some conditions. They suggested that the Alaska Wolf Planning team (who had drawn up the original plan) be reinstated to make further recommendations about wolf management.

Over the last few years Alaska has ended statewide government wolf-control

programs, banned poisons and aerial-hunting, ended bounty payments and introduced regulations to control wolf hunting and trapping. There are several large National Parks within which wolves enjoy complete protection. The wolf is not endangered. Quite the reverse; but this does not mean that culling is necessarily the right course of action.

Indiscriminate killing disrupts the complex social life of wolves. When a pack is disrupted by the death of its alpha leaders it may split up, all its members dispersing to become sexually active as they found new packs in other areas. Russian research suggests that continual pressure on the wolf population does not necessarily reduce numbers at all. Instead, killing wolves may simply worsen relations with farmers. Orphaned immature wolves like those of the first

White wolves occur in cold northerly latitudes, both in North America and in Russia. The white hair shafts contain air pockets instead of the pigment melanin, so the coat has greater insulation properties as well as being lighter in weight.

Nine Mile Pack in Montana, may hunt domestic stock rather than natural prey because their parents were killed before they had time to instil normal hunting behavior in their offspring. If wolves have to be culled to reduce numbers, it seems the entire family must be removed together.

It is extremely sad that the two qualities that we most admire in the wolf, that of the bold, cunning hunter and the careful, loving parent, are the first casualties in our long-running war with this splendid predator. It is easy to admire the wolf from afar, from the pages of a picture book, from the sights of camera or binoculars. In countries where wolves are common, their management is a nightmare. One line of argument current in American conservation circles suggests that we should quit the killing and let wolf populations find their own natural level. No doubt they would do so, but research suggests that the populations of both wolves and their prey would stabilize at a lower density than exists at present, scattered thinly over the land.

Almost everywhere, wolves and men compete directly with each other for control of the ungulates that transform the sunlight locked up in the cellulose of indigestible plants into food that meat-eaters can use. Competition is part of nature, but this conflict is unnaturally biased, weighted by weaponry in favor of mankind. It is too late to talk of a natural ecosystem uninfluenced by human needs. We do not understand nature, but like a child at the wheel of a runaway truck, we have been left in the driving seat. National Parks exist only because we want them to. In the future, that's the way it's going to be with wolves too.

A parent instilling discipline into one of the pups. Hunting by man causes trauma within the pack, upsetting the delicate social relationships which naturally govern wolf numbers.

Opposite: Wolves appeal to animal lovers, many of whom protest strongly against wolf hunting. In some areas, populations are dwindling and wolves urgently need protection. However, where they are numerous, wolf hunting is encouraged.

113

CHAPTER TEN

RUSSIAN ROULETTE

Powerful three-axle Gaza and Ural trucks, two LAZ and three UAZ buses, plus our "landrovers." Eight vehicles . . . everyone was armed to the teeth. Cartridges on belts crossed bandit-style, hacking knives, binoculars, flares. This "mechanized army" could lay waste to the taiga with its hardware alone, but of course everyone also carried into the field his rifle, one or two barrels. Hundreds of barrels . . . I tried to estimate how many shots our "army" would fire, how much wildlife they would kill, but I gave up: we were one of hundreds of big-city enterprises going out today into "nature's bosom."

Vladimir Sapozhnikov. From Boris Komarov, The Destruction of Nature in the Soviet Union (M. E. Sharpe Inc., New York, 1980)

Until recently the Soviet Union extended to more than 13.6 million square miles (22 million sq km) and within its borders lay 18 percent of the land surface of our planet. This is a vastness that defeats the imagination. Now the USSR is no more and this territory is administered by the governments of many independent states. The fortunes of wolves, as we have seen, can never be separated from the politics of man. Within the former Soviet Union there are now more wolves than anywhere else on earth. They range across the whole of Russia and its erstwhile dominions, with many populations surviving at near natural densities.

This is not because Russians – or their neighbours – are fond of wolves. The wolf is distrusted as much here as anywhere, but so far wolves have not been ousted in spite of several campaigns of savage persecution. More than 1.5 million wolves have been killed during the last seventy years, but wolves are as numerous today as ever. The population is so astonishingly resilient, that Russia's leading wolf expert, Professor Dimitry Bibikov, has come to believe that hunting does not necessarily reduce numbers but can have the opposite effect in some circumstances, leading to changes in wolf behavior which increase their rate of breeding.

Wolves can be found occupying an astonishing range of habitats in the former USSR. The frozen wastes of the tundra are their northern limit, but wolves exist throughout the taiga tree-belt and are even found roaming over farmland on the open steppe. The mountains of the Caucasus, Tian-Shan and the Altai are major strongholds and wolves are still to be found in the Asiatic desert regions. From

115

north to south, from east to west, the territory of the wolf stretches right across the continent from the icy wastes of the Kola Peninsula in the north-west, to the exotic forests of Ussuriland, on the coast of the Pacific.

Conditions in the USSR during the twentieth century have been generally favorable towards wolves because the activities of man have ensured a glut of prey, both wild and domestic. Tundra wolves depend on reindeer for winter food and two-thirds of the world's reindeer are Russian. Nine hundred thousand of them, are the same species as wild North American caribou, *Rangifer tarandus*. The rest are a domestic subspecies and include tens of thousands of feral reindeer which have escaped from captivity. The biggest herds can be found on the Taimyr Peninsula, where numbers exceed 430,000. In all there are at least 4 million reindeer in the Russian Arctic today.

When the collectivization of reindeer herds began in the late 1920s it caused great distress among the nomadic pastoralists of the Arctic whose unique way of life was destroyed overnight. Confined within farm boundaries, the reindeer could not follow sensible migration routes and some years, when snow fell heavily, up to 70 percent died. The farms' loss was the wolves' gain. For political reasons the collective farms were not dismantled and the mismanagement continued. Softened by their relationship with man, domestic reindeer cannot defend themselves effectively against wolves. They stand still rather than run and seem unable to kick out at their attackers which sometimes kill large numbers in a single raid.

In the dense forests of the taiga, wolves prey on reindeer (caribou) and elk (moose), Arctic hare and beaver, just like their North American counterparts. The Russian taiga is immense, over 4,000 miles (6,400 km) across; more than twice the size of the Amazon rainforest and very much bigger than the taiga of North America. This boreal forest (named after Boreas, the god of the North Wind in Greek mythology) is made up of pines, larches, spruces and firs. Wolves can be found thinly spread throughout the tree-belt at densities of around one wolf to 620 miles (1,000 km) but they prefer to live around the edge of the forest, particularly in the open conifer woodlands of the north where the snow is constantly blown away by the wind and hunting is easier.

Until the twentieth century much of the taiga was hardly touched by man but deforestation is accelerating rapidly. The Russians need money and there is an international demand for timber – at the right price. As the chainsaws cut into the dark heart of the wood, the recently cleared land provides better habitat for wild ungulates such as elk, deer and wild boar. Their numbers are increasing, which is in turn boosting the population of wolves who dwell among the trees and causing major changes in their distribution.

To the south of the taiga lies the wild and windswept Russian steppe. Until the twentieth century it was a seemingly limitless area of grassland, stretching from Hungary and the Lower Danube through the Ukraine and the southern part of European Russia and Western Siberia and still further, reaching to the very edge of Mongolia and China. However, since the nineteenth century in the European part of Russia, the steppe has been heavily exploited – often disastrously – for agriculture. Only 6 square miles (3.7 sq km) of the original feather-grass habitat remain unploughed (lying within the reserve of Askaniya-Nova), and erosion is taking its toll of the surrounding black soils that stretch as far as the eye can see in every direction. Yet in spite of the ecologically damaging changes that have been

Previous page: Wolf populations in Eurasia have fluctuated wildly during the twentieth century. In many countries wolves are now entirely rare, or extirpated.

wreaked on the steppe and the fact that the wild ungulate population has shrunk to insignificant levels, wolves continue to thrive. They have adapted to the changes and now they concentrate, not in wild areas, but around villages and farms.

It is not simply domestic stock that lures the wolf towards human settlement. Rodents thrive around farms where they enjoy an all-year-round supply of food, especially cereal crops. Voles and suslik populations are booming, particularly in Zanolgje and West Kazachstan where they are estimated to number hundreds of millions. These rodents make a welcome addition to the wolves' diet.

The bobak or Steppe marmot is about the size of a small cat and in arid areas of steppe and desert, where large prey like Goitred gazelle is scarce and fleet of foot, wolves are not choosy. They will even eat gerbils, although it needs to be said that the Great gerbil is a monster compared to the familiar children's pet, growing up to 8 inches (20 cm) long. The Common hamster, a chunky cousin of the Golden hamster, makes another satisfying snack.

The arid landscapes of the north Caspian Sea boast larger prey. The Saiga antelope looks rather like a sheep or goat, with the addition of a peculiar, trumpet-shaped nose. This appendage is designed to keep dust out of the saiga's

In Kazakhstan, wolves are traditionally hunted with a large subspecies of Golden eagle. To avoid being bitten, the bird must make its kill by grasping the wolf over the nose with one foot while it sinks the talons of the other into the neck. Wolves are not the eagle's natural prey and only the most powerful females have the strength to hunt them. Until recently wolf hunting was very popular in Kazakhstan where, encouraged by Soviet bounties, it held the status of a national sport.

Wolves can be found in all regions of the former USSR, even in the arid areas of the Steppe. Although numbers have fallen sharply as a result of the use of modern weapons and helicopters during periodic campaigns to control wolves, bounty payments are no longer available from Moscow and Russian biologists predict a rapid recovery.

Opposite: Adult wolves teach their pups to beware the drone of aircraft. In some areas of Russia it is reported that wolves no longer howl for fear of man.

lungs, but it droops so far over the muzzle that the saiga has to wrinkle it out of the way to eat. A contemporary of the woolly mammoth, saiga antelope once grazed right across Europe and North America, from Britain to Alaska. The last herds of Russian saiga were devastated by overhunting during the eighteenth and nineteenth centuries – the meat is delicious – but captive breeding techniques and strict protection between 1950 and 1980 rescued the species from extinction. This was a great conservation success for Russia, and for a while the herds numbered more than 2 million. Wolves traditionally prey on saiga, particularly on their newborn young, and they play an important part in managing the herds. However, in the political confusion of the 1990s, protection has waned. The horns of the male saiga are valuable because they are used in oriental medicine. During the last three years the saiga population has dropped by 90 percent as poachers have destroyed the herds.

Driven by the changeover to a market economy, there has been a tremendous escalation in poaching throughout the former Soviet Union, according to a recent report of the Theriological Society of the Russian Acadamy of Sciences. The situation is particularly bad in the Far East where the proximity to the Chinese border creates a ready market for animal products. In Primorsky (Vladivostok) province, the price of a tiger-skin was reported to be 10,000 dollars, while announcements about the sale of pelts and the parts of animals required for use in Chinese medicine continue to be made on radio and television, as well as posted in the streets. In 1992 about eighty Brown bears and thirty Polar bears were killed to obtain their bile, a medicinal substance that fetches 8 dollars a gram. There seems no way to halt the killing. The leopard is extremely rare – perhaps already lost – and the Siberian tiger is in great danger.

Deep in the oak forests of Ussuriland that lie between China and the Pacific, wolves still depend on wild food such as roe deer and a local race of wild boar. They have always been numerous in Russia's Far East, and during the 1980s

around 145,000 wolf-pelts were exported each year from this area. The figure is higher now, for wolf-pelts from all over the former Soviet Union are finding their way to the markets of the East to be exchanged for Toyota cars.

As entrepreneurs struggle to exploit the new market economy, damage to the environment is accelerating. The only fully protected areas lie within the Soviet system of *zapovedniki* or nature reserves which are recognized as one of the most important conservation networks in the world. Many were set up to protect or rescue rare species such as the saiga antelope, the wild ass or the Russian desmen (an aquatic mole). On Wrangel Island in the Arctic Ocean, wolves prowl among Polar bears, walruses, Snow geese and Ross's roseate gull, whilst the Taimyr Peninsula is particularly famous for the rare Red-breasted goose (*Branta ruficollis*) which breeds only in Siberia. Keeping a balance between endangered species and wolves has been difficult for Soviet biologists and wardens. Wildlife reserves offer wolves only limited protection. Although they hold territories in ninety-six of the 106 reserves, the status of wolves is simply unknown in fifty of them, while they are actively controlled at forty-one sites. It is not only that biologists are committed to the protection of other species. One of the problems with reserves such as Oka, Mordovian, Khopyor and Central Forest is that they are too small to sustain a healthy wolf-pack. When the offspring disperse, they are forced to prey on domestic animals pastured on adjoining land. Wolves stay within the boundaries of only the largest reserves, those that cover 310–620 square miles (500–1,000 sq km) such as the Caucasian, Pechyora-Ilych and Altai Reserves.

Folktales from nineteenth-century Russia – and earlier – tell of unlimited numbers of wolves and describe hungry packs chasing troikas or sleighs during particularly cold winters. Although conservationists like to emphasize the harmless nature of the wolf, recently researched archive material from the 1940s and 1950s paints a rather different picture.

Wolves traditionally thrive when human populations are in distress, so it is no surprise to learn that wolf numbers rose steeply during the First and Second World Wars when the deaths of millions of men led to a deterioration in standards of agriculture. By the end of the hostilities, it was calculated that the unchecked wolf population had swollen to between 150,000 and 200,000 animals. In 1924 and 1925 over a million head of cattle were reported killed by wolves. Predation was particularly heavy in the lower Volga (2.2 percent lost), Siberia (1.6 percent lost) and Kazakhstan (1.5 percent lost). Human survivors of the war turned their lethal attention to the wolves, as soldiers must have done after every conflict throughout history.

In the 1940s, the wolf population peaked for a second time at around 200,000. Again, ruthless control measures were instigated. In 1944, 43,000 wolves were killed in Russia, while the figure for the whole of the USSR totaled an astonishing 62,000 for the year. Wolves continued to be dispatched at the rate of about 40,000 to 50,000 annually for the next fifteen years. By the mid-1960s, the battle was counted won and the Soviet authorities relaxed the annual cull to 15,000, for the official intention was always control, not extirpation. In spite of the years of relentless slaughter, wolves could still be found over most Soviet territory. Between 1968 and 1972 the Soviet wolf population reached the lowest point in its history. As numbers dropped to 50,000, their vast range broke up temporarily into discontinuous blocks, particularly in the European part of the Soviet bloc.

Half the land in the Baltic area became free of wolves and the population was much reduced in Byelorussia, central Russia and the Ukraine.

For a short while biologists thought the wolf problem had been resolved. Wolves existed in healthy numbers, but the population was not so high as to cause farmers distress. However, climatic conditions in the USSR were favorable to wildlife. Populations of prey were expanding and at the end of the 1970s, perhaps in response to this, the wolves made yet another spectacular recovery to peak in the 1980s at around 120,000. Wolves were now so numerous that rabies became a danger. A public outcry sparked off another intensive campaign of shooting, poisoning, trapping and hunting, aided this time by an army of motorized sledges, aircraft and helicopters. More than 32,000 wolves were killed during 1979 alone. There was no particular strategy behind the killing. Without reference to ecological considerations it rapidly turned into a campaign to exterminate the wolf.

Helicopters made certain subspecies particularly vulnerable. It was a simple matter to find Tundra wolves and Desert wolves in their characteristic open habitats. At the end of the 1960s it was estimated that only thirty Tundra wolves survived on the Kola Peninsula. Most had fled their native country to hide from the helicopters among the trees of the taiga. Here they bred with Taiga wolves and so the genetic difference between the two was compromised. Despite some recovery there are no more than 2,000 Tundra wolves left throughout the former USSR today. The Desert wolf has been reduced to a population of around 7,000, while the Central Asian wolf (*Canis lupus campestris*, the name means "wolf of the open plains") has become rare in the European part of Russia.

In spite of public concern, the killing continued until 1990, for it was in the interests of many officials to divert public funds into hunting for their own private profit. A bounty of 150 roubles for a female, 100 roubles for a male and 50 roubles for a pup was enough to encourage entrepreneurs who made incentive payments to corrupt officials to gain access to State transport. Over 36,000 pelts were taken in 1988, more than twice that of the previous decade. Not only wolves were killed, some airborne hunters made use of official facilities to kill game animals too. Native hunters were excluded from this aerial bonanza, which deprived them of their traditional harvest – a modest and sustainable yield of deer and wolf-skins. In Taymir, local hunters were reported to have muttered, "Perhaps we should fire our rifles at the helicopter!"

The situation was exacerbated by the distribution to farms of a large quantity of poisoned baits which killed other species such as Arctic foxes, wolverines, Red foxes and Golden eagles in alarming numbers. However, the tide of public opinion was turning and in the changing political circumstances of the USSR this voice was being heard: the poisoning program was curtailed in 1985.

The public fear of rabies has been an important factor in the debate on wolf control. Rabies is not a problem in wolves where the population is low and, these days, the wolf is the principal virus-carrier mainly in the Asiatic regions of the former USSR. In other areas foxes and racoon are far more dangerous for they transmit the virus to domestic dogs and cats, which brings this deadly disease into contact with man.

The control of rabies in Russia does not demand the extirpation of wolves. Wolves may, in fact, reduce the incidence of rabies by keeping the fox and racoon populations down. However, the density of the wolf population seems to be

Our old fear of wolves may be closely connected to our fear of rabies. Russian research suggests that in areas where wolves are particularly numerous, a higher percentage seem to carry the virus than in other places. The vast majority of rabid wolves do not go mad or attack people. However, in Eurasia this kind of tragedy is still possible and is a strong argument for controlling wolf populations.

critical. Information gathered by Professor Bibikov and others in Russia suggests that in the present conditions, few wolves are rabid. However, in the semi-desert of Kazakhstan where wolves are still numerous, seventeen out of fifty-four wolves studied during 1972 to 1978 turned out to be carriers of the virus.

Moved by several tragic incidents from rural parts of their dominions, the Czars of the nineteenth century encouraged physicians to pay close attention to the work of Louis Pasteur. Records show that from 1763 to 1891 wolves attacked 218 people of whom seventy-five (34 percent) died of rabies. Pasteur's research in Paris demonstrated that once symptoms of the disease emerged, no cure was possible. That is still the case. However, the inoculation of victims to prevent the onset of sickness is effective, and this is fortunate for, even today, human rabies still occurs in many countries around the world.

When the wolf population began to peak for the third time this century, during the 1970s, wolves were particularly abundant in the Voronezh region. Early on the morning of February 8, 1980 in the village of Soleny, a rabid wolf managed to

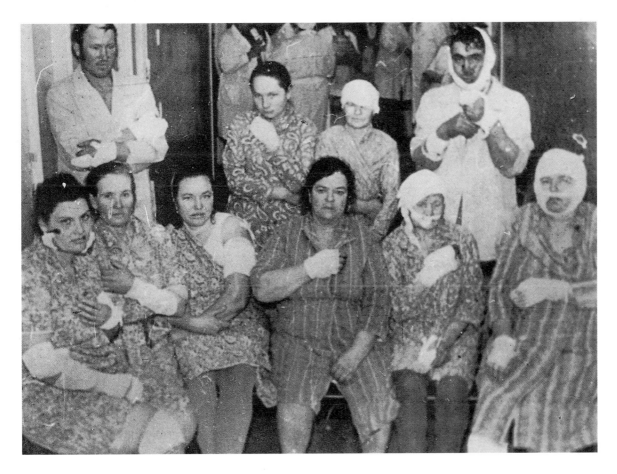

Within the space of one and a half hours on the morning of February 8, 1980, ten peasants were attacked by a male rabid wolf near Soleny village in the Voronezh Region of Russia. The victims were airlifted to Voronezh Hospital where they received intensive anti-rabies treatment. Although three were badly mauled and considered to be in a serious condition, all survived.

Although government veterinarians disagree with the practice, peasants in Russia continue to dispose of dead livestock by dumping the bodies in open pits, like this one near Novokhopyorski in the south-west of the Voronezh Region. It is hoped that care for domestic animals will improve under free market conditions. Meanwhile, there continues to be plenty of carrion for wolves.

bite ten people within the space of an hour and a half. Although three were badly injured, they all survived after intensive treatment. Numerous wolf attacks were also reported from the Bryansk region where one family (in February 1982) described how a rabid wolf leaped into their sleigh. Eleven victims are recorded by V. Adamovich in L'vov in 1991, as well as further incidents from Byelorussia, the Chernigov and Guryev regions. These well-documented reports of attacks by animals subsequently examined and found to be carriers of the virus, suggest that wolves can still play a role in the transmission of rabies to man, even in European Russia.

There are no simple answers. The danger lies not only in burgeoning wolf populations, but in those recently brought to the verge of extinction by high-tech control methods. When males cannot find female wolves with which to mate, they couple with domestic and feral dogs to produce hybrid litters. When hybrids become rabid, they are far more dangerous to people than wolves living natural lives, for they can wander into villages unremarked. Although records show that wolves can be dangerous, in over 98 percent of cases rabies is transmitted by domestic pets who have acquired the virus from foxes.

Russian scientists suggest that when wolves are forced to live in stressful circumstances, continually molested by hunters, they react in a number of interesting ways to guarantee their survival. The pups mature faster and leave the dangerous area of the den sooner. The timing of the estrus in young wolves is shifted so that if the alpha female is killed during estrus or early gestation, she can be replaced by a subdominant female who is immediately able to mate. If both alpha wolves are lost, their places are taken by younger animals, so the wolf-pack still manages to produce a litter and is not exterminated or driven from its range.

In cases when the entire pack was killed, scientists noticed that when the territory was recolonized – maybe a year or two later – the newcomers used the same dens as the previous occupants.

Stress seems to have changed the social structure of packs in several regions of the former USSR. Scientists working in the Taimyr, Karelia and Altai regions have found packs in which two or even three pregnant females or females in estrus were found to be coexisting. Survivors of the last campaign to exterminate the species have learned to avoid danger and have evolved new ways of evading pursuit and hiding from man. It is said that this new breed of wolf can distinguish between the noise of "safe" and "dangerous" aircraft; they have learned to scatter as the helicopters descend; they have learned to escape the firepower of pursuing vehicles by crossing the track to the driver's side, thus making shooting difficult. The maneuver, known as "skip the rope" in local slang, allows the wolf to escape while the driver performs a U-turn. Professor Bibikov comments: "Severe repression . . . had the same effect as behavioral selection: silly animals were the first to die." Under relentless pressure from hunters, the Russian wolves have become more intelligent, cautious and adaptable in their struggle to survive. Some wolf-packs have fallen silent in the face of persecution and they suppress the joy of howling in their pups.

In 1988 it was calculated that there were only 29,000 wolves left in Russia – perhaps 50,000 overall – but in 1993 all the signs indicate that wolves are recovering their numbers yet again. The population has risen to at least 40,000 wolves in Russia during the last five years, and it is thought that there is now a population of approximately 100,000 ranging throughout the former Soviet Union which can only increase over the next few years.

Changing to a market-led economy will shift the onus of wolf control from the State to private individuals, mostly farmers and hunters. The management of the wolf as a game animal will be organized by local authorities and hunting societies. There will be no more bounties and no more aerial hunting. Without these incentives, the killing will slow down and wolf numbers are bound to rise. But will the wolf population stabilize? With wildlife at the mercy of hunting societies and poachers, it is likely that natural prey will soon disappear. The combination presents an alarming scenario which can only end badly, provoking yet another panic-driven crusade of slaughter.

Russian biologists are convinced that mass-killing is not the way to find a balance between wolf and man. The former USSR is so large and its wolf habitats so varied that control must be tailored to precise local conditions. If the wolf is extirpated from any area, its ecological niche will be swiftly occupied by packs of feral dogs which cause far more damage to both wild and domestic stock.

Now retired after a lifetime studying wolves in the former Soviet Union, Professor Bibikov drew my attention to the words of Paul Errington: "the wolf problem is so complex, so embedded in sinister extremes, so muddled up by wrong concepts and half-truth . . . that most of the public sees the only way out . . . in getting rid of it once and for all. The latter is an awful oversimplification fraught with the possibilities of grave mistakes."

He adds: "These prophetic words should always be remembered, since rude, short-sighted intrusion into wildlife can produce, instead of one wolf problem created by ourselves, a number of more troublesome ones . . ."

ON THE EDGE IN EURASIA

*Wolves, like all other wildlife, have a right to exist in a wild state. This right is in
no way related to their known value to mankind. Instead it derives from the
right of all living creatures to co-exist with man as part of natural ecosystems.*

From the IUCN Manifesto on Wolf Conservation

Teeming populations of Russian wolves have long acted as a reservoir from
which dispersing individuals could spread into neighboring countries. In this
way fresh blood has invigorated European populations which might otherwise
have died out. If this vital link remains unbroken and Russian wolves increase in
numbers as predicted, those countries that accept the wolf's presence are
guaranteed a modest population for some time to come.

Wolves with family ties extending far into the Caucasus have established two
small strongholds in eastern Poland. Several packs survive in the north among
the Masurian Lakes and in the Biebrza Marshes. Nearby, Poland's border with
Russia is regularly penetrated by newcomers who trickle through the forests and
mires of the Bialowieza National Park. This terrain has always been wild, so
impenetrable that during the last war it provided a last refuge to nationalists and
refugees from the Nazis. A small part of the Bialowieza remains completely
untouched by man, the very last scrap of a primeval forest that once stretched
right across Europe. Despite its historic fascination, the wolves are not found in
the pristine forest but in the surrounding managed areas where timber-felling has
created airy glades and provides grazing for red deer and Europe's most
important herd of wild bison.

Hunting is big business in Poland. For hundreds of years the forests have been
carefully managed, with the aim of producing a high density of deer together
with stags bearing large trophy antlers. Hitler and his deputy Goering, the
founder of the Gestapo, were so delighted with the quality of the hunting in
eastern Poland that they toyed with the idea of removing the entire human
population in order to turn the area into a game preserve for the Reich. Germans
are still valued clients. Heavy red deer antlers, weighing 6 pounds (10 kg) or
more, can fetch as much as 10,000 dollars, so the management of deer is of
serious economic importance.

Throughout most of its history in Poland the wolf has been regarded as a pest.

A sportsman proudly exhibits his trophy, a wolf killed near the Bialowieza National Park, Poland. In Europe, the status of 'game animal' gives stronger protection than that of 'vermin'.

Previous page: Eurasian wolves occupy a wide range of habitats but like their North American counterparts, they thrive best in remote areas, far from man. Wolves survive on the arid Russian steppe as well as the Gobi desert.

A post-war campaign reduced the population to only 100, but in 1977 the wolf was elevated to the status of a game animal and limited protection improved its chances of survival. The population has recovered and now numbers about 1,000. This has alarmed hunters, some of whom are demanding its complete extirpation. Fortunately for wolves, German hard currency is what counts and some clients prefer the excitement of shooting wolves to killing deer. They pay handsomely to hunt by the traditional "battue" method.

A battue involves a great deal of work. Brightly colored flags are attached to long lengths of rope which are coiled in readiness. During the weeks leading up to the hunt, the foresters keep a sharp look-out for wolf footprints. The managed forest at Bialowieza is divided into squares separated by a grid of forest roads so that it is possible to work out where the resident wolf-pack may be found. If the tracks leading into one of the squares do not also lead out, the wolves are undoubtedly within that square. On the day of the hunt the decorated rope is hung around the block and beaters begin to walk through the trees, driving the wolves forward to where the huntsman waits with his gun. The organization is elaborate, the outcome of the whole affair so inevitable that it is hard to see how sportsmanship comes into it at all.

As pressure from the battue increases, the frightened wolf runs first to one side of the block of trees and then to the other. At each turn it is brought up short by a fragile barrier of flags. Why can't the wolf leap the rope and run to freedom? The caution that arms all wolves in their relations with man works against it in this case. It dare not. Towards the end, a forester removes the rope to lure the wolf out in front of the client's jeep. He could shoot it from the passenger seat – but it is considered good manners to descend. Afterwards, photographs are taken of the intrepid hunter and his prey.

Poland's largest wolf population is found among the alpine meadows of the Bieszczady Mountains which are part of the Carpathian range in the south-east corner of the country. This region used to be farmed by pastoralists who once grazed large herds of sheep and goats on the high meadows, but these communities were abandoned during the Second World War. Now this rugged land has been reclaimed by nature, perhaps for ever. Nowhere in Poland is so rich in wildlife as the 30,000 acres (12,000 hectares) protected by the Bieszczady National Park. The mountains are covered by a forest of beech fir trees (*Fagetum capaticum*), and wolves share the region with endangered predators such as Brown bear, lynx and wildcat. Red and roe deer form the bulk of their prey but there are also wild boar and European bison in the forest.

Wolves pass freely across the border into the state of **Slovakia** (separated from Czechoslovakia in 1993) where about 300 wolves occur, mostly in the mountainous area along the Polish border. Around 120 wolves – well over one-third of the population – are killed every year in this region. The very survival of wolves in Slovakia implies that the dead are continually replaced by immigrants from Poland and the Ukraine, following natural pathways through the Carpathian Mountains.

Until recently it was thought that wolves were only occasional visitors to **Hungary**, spilling over from the Ukraine and Romania, but recently two breeding populations have been discovered. One lies in the north-east near the border with the Ukraine and the other is situated in south-central Hungary where wolves feed on livestock as well as red deer and mouflon. An endangered

A wolf lies dead after a hunt in which the 'battue' method was used. Driven by beaters towards the guns, the wolf is too frightened to jump across the red flags to freedom.

species in Hungary, the wolf is protected in so far as a license is required to comply with the law.

Further south, following the border with the Ukraine, a vigorous population numbering about 2,500 wolves survives in **Romania**. Once again, their stronghold lies in the Carpathian Mountains where they feed on roe deer and wild boar. Wolves are not protected in Romania. Quite the reverse; the government has been paying a bounty on about 250 wolves a year which are also trapped for their fur. Since the overthrow of Ceauşescu in December 1989 the newly formed Directorate for Conservation and Ecological Rehabilitation in the Ministry of Environment has increased the network of protected areas in Romania. Most of the forests will continue to be managed by government for economic production, although Romanian scientists are forging links with colleagues in other countries which may lead to the development of new conservation policies.

Although wolves traditionally thrive when humans are fully occupied killing each other, the war that has torn **Yugoslavia** apart may have had a catastrophic effect on wildlife in the region. Although small, **Croatia** has a particularly rich heritage of natural habitats, including several rare old forests. It is claimed that the Serbian army has deliberately ruined UNESCO Biosphere Reserves such as Velebit and Biokovo, the National Park Plitvice Lakes (a World Heritage Monument), the Krka River National Park and the Kopacki Rit Reserve, which is a refuge for several hundred species of migratory birds. Until recently the mountainous regions of Croatia held significant populations of bear and lynx as well as wolves. Croatian biologists claim that Serbian soldiers armed with machine-guns are indiscriminately killing every living thing that moves in pursuit of an official policy of total destruction.

Before the war started, the Yugoslavian wolf population stood at around 2,000, found mostly in the mountains of the south-west and north-east. It was estimated that 400 wolves occupied areas in the central republic of Bosnia-Hercegovina. The population was already in steep decline. In 1969 over 2,000 wolves were "harvested" and during the early 1980s more than 1,000 a year were culled. Wolves could be killed by anyone, by any means, at any time in Yugoslavia. This open season appears to have been extended to include Croatians and the ethnic minorities of the broken State. In the present situation, wolves figure rather low on the political agenda.

Barely 100 wolves survive in **Bulgaria** where they have been largely replaced by a vigorous population of jackals (*Canis aureus*) which is decimating flocks of domestic sheep, pigs and chickens. Normally the presence of wolves would inhabit the jackals' activities, but with the larger canids absent, the smaller dogs have taken over the niche of top predator, and they are hunting wild populations of fallow and red deer.

The population in **Albania** is unknown, but in **Greece** conservationists are trying to save the last wolves of the country that 2,000 years ago was the cradle of Europe's most powerful wolf legends. In theory wolves are legally protected, for Greece is a signatory to the Treaty of Bern, but although there are no more than 500 wolves left, they are being shot and poisoned at the rate of about 100 a year. Unfortunately wolves in Greece are largely dependent on livestock for prey because human overhunting has almost destroyed the population of wild ungulates. The World Wide Fund for Nature is active in Greece, but education is not enough. The law will continue to be ignored until a fair system of compensation can be set up. Until then the wolf will continue to be shot on sight. The wolf's best chance of survival seems to lie within protected areas such as the National Parks of Vikos-Aoos and Vallia Calda in the Northern Pindos; in the primeval forest of Zagradenia in the Rodopi range; in the forest of Dadia and the wetlands of the Evros delta; within the Oeta National Park in the mountain range of Ghiona-Vardoussia-Oeta and in the region of Mount Koziakas.

Although wolves are not protected by law in **Turkey,** they occur everywhere from the Mediterranean coast to Eastern Anatolia. Farmers and hunters like to kill them but hunting is forbidden inside National Parks and nature reserves, afforestation and reforestation areas, forest and soil conservation areas and areas devoted to the breeding of wild animals. These protected areas add up to 16 percent of Turkey, an area of at least 80,600 square miles (130,000 sq km). The Turkish wolf population is invigorated by links with wolves in mountainous areas of **Georgia, Armenia, Azerbaijan** and north-west **Iran** where wolf populations have always been high.

Wolves can be found everywhere in **Iran,** thinly distributed over coastal plains, sandy deserts, rocky foothills and steppe as well as in deciduous forest. They are killed where they prey on domestic sheep, but there are enough reserves and National Parks in which wolves breed unmolested to guarantee their survival. Due to the large size of the wolves' territories, they are seldom seen by shepherds and are of so little significance that Iranian children are generally left to mind the flocks and herds in most parts of Iran. The area of the Arasbaran Protected Region in north-west Iran is notably different. Here the only natural prey is ibex, but these wild goat-antelope inhabit high mountainous areas, too steep and dangerous even for wolves. At lower altitudes, however, there are up to 100,000 domestic sheep and goats which offer an easy alternative. Villagers frequently encounter wolves, who are notorious for attacking the same flock several times in one day. Only adult men or strong teenaged boys are allowed to be shepherds in this area. Large dogs are kept as a defense, although wolves sometimes kill the dogs if they stray too far from their masters. During winter, when the sheep and goats are safely shut away in barns, wolves are often seen prowling around villages and farms. Although newspapers in Iran sometimes describe wolves attacking humans – thirteen villagers were reported mauled in 1989 – these are usually isolated accounts involving rabid animals. Most are grossly exaggerated. Even in Iran, healthy wolves are generally too frightened of man to attack, even when they are starving.

The desert-living wolves of the Middle East are not only much smaller than their northern cousins, they are almost entirely silent. Iranian wolves are seldom heard to howl. The wolves of **Iraq, Syria, Israel, Jordan** and the **Lebanon** live as shadows at the edge of human civilization. Overhunting has destroyed the wildlife of much of the Middle East and overgrazing by sheep and goats is accelerating the process of desertification in many areas. **Israel** is the only country in the Middle East that directly protects wolves, but some countries such as **Jordan, Oman** and the **United Arab Emirates** have introduced restrictions on hunting which will, in time, improve the management of wild areas.

Although the majority of **Israel's** wolves were killed by an anti-rabies program during the British Mandatory period (1918–48), four physically different populations of wolf have managed to survive, albeit in low numbers. There are two types of South Asian wolf (*Canis lupus pallipes*) living in the lush area of Central Israel. One of these is medium-colored and slightly heavier than the other, which is a pale wolf, occasionally found in the Negev Desert. During the summer months when temperatures are high, they hunt at night but during the winter these wolves are active by day and are often seen resting on hilltops.

Larger than the desert wolves and conspicuously darker-colored, another subspecies can be found in Upper Galilee and the Golan Heights. Weighing over 66 pounds (30 kg) this wolf is probably descended from European stock, the subspecies *Canis lupus lupus*. Unfortunately for the long-term future of this small group of fascinating predators, they have developed a taste for veal. In an effort to reconcile the differences between farmers and wolves the Israel Nature Reserves Authority is providing the herdsmen with specially trained guard dogs.

On the **Arabian Peninsula**, in Southern Sinai, the far south of **Israel** and in southern **Jordan**, the smallest wolf in the world makes a living at the edge of the desert. The Pale desert wolf (*Canis lupus arabs*) weighs just under 40 pounds (18 kg) and is so much more delicate than the North American timber wolf that it is hard to believe they are the same species. While Asian wolves (*Canis lupus*

pallipes) hunt in a pack to bring down prey the size of a donkey, the Pale desert wolf hunts alone, feeding on rodents, foxes and dogs. Like many wolves in areas where wild prey is scarce, it scavenges on dead stock, road casualties and rubbish dumps. Wolves used to be common animals in Arabia. Although they still occur over much of the peninsula, the population is now very low. Desert wolves are animals of open country, fairly well adapted to arid conditions. They escape the heat by digging deep dens, but as they cannot survive without water they do not wander far into the great sand deserts.

Even smaller and more endangered, the Ethiopian wolf is so unwolflike that it was known as the Simian jackal until the International Union for the Conservation of Nature (IUCN) Canid Specialist Group decided – on genetic evidence – that its name should be changed. The new name *Canis simensis* gives it the taxonomic stature of an entirely new wolf species. Endemic to the highlands of **Ethiopia**, only 500 are thought to exist, which makes it the world's most endangered canid. While most threatened wolf populations are very thinly spread over a large area, the Ethiopian wolf is vulnerable because over half its population is concentrated inside Bale National Park. The local Oromo people

One of the last wolves in Bulgaria, where hunting has reduced the population to only 100. Unfortunately for farmers, jackals have taken over the wolves' niche and are causing far more damage to livestock than their predecessors.

133

The Pale desert wolf Canis lupus arabs *from Saudi Arabia is the smallest subspecies of Gray wolf weighing only 40lb (18kg). Slender in its thin coat, it lives on the margins of the great Arabian sand dunes, one of the world's most arid areas.*

are normally tolerant of their rare wolves which feed mainly on rodents rather than domestic stock; however, following the overthrow of Mengistu's government in May 1991, automatic weapons were sold to the tribespeople by deserting soldiers. Wild animals were used as shooting targets and several Ethiopian wolves from the Park were killed.

It is estimated that no more than 2,000 wolves survive on the entire **Indian subcontinent**, where the Asian Gray wolf (*Canis lupus pallipes*) is slowly losing the battle for survival. The figure could be much lower. Although these wolves can be found scattered over a wide area, the population is subject to heavy persecution, while agriculture and land development continue to reduce the natural habitat. In some places wolves have been totally extirpated.

Unlike the Asian wolves of Iran, Asian wolves in India howl frequently; behavior which has been helpful to scientists who are trying to estimate the size of their population. Indian wolves take a wide range of prey, depending on the type of habitat, which includes blackbuck, wild boar, cattle, sheep and goats, as well as rodents. Their increasing reliance on livestock brings them into conflict

with pastoralists. Older men of the Waghries and Bharvads tribes have reported that, while wolves were quite common during their youth, none have been seen during the past few decades.

National Parks and nature reserves represent the wolf's best chance for survival in India. However, many of these Parks are hardly nature reserves at all, being heavily used by domestic stock which reduces the grazing available to wild ungulates. India's reserves are underfunded and there are not enough wardens to protect them. In Velavadar National Park in Gujarat Province in the north-west of India, an 8-acre (20-hectare) area surrounding a key wolf rendezvous site has recently been purchased from a local farmer (with funds from "Wolf Symposium 92" in Canada) to prevent the continual disturbance caused by agricultural activities.

One would expect the wolf population to be more numerous in **Ladakh**, situated at the northernmost tip of India in the State of Jammu and Kashmir. One of the most sparsely populated areas of India, Ladakh is a mountainous region between 6,000 and 12,000 feet (3,000 and 6,000 m) in altitude. On the edge of

The population of the Asian wolf Canis lupus pallipes *is thinly distributed from the Middle East through Pakistan and India to the borders of China and Tibet.*

135

Mongolian wolves have suffered as a result of a Government campaign to limit their numbers, however canids are important predators of rodents on the high altitude plains of Central Asia. The uncontrolled killing of wolves and foxes is said to be responsible for recent rodent plagues which have caused considerable damage to agriculture.

the Tibetan plateau, it is an arid land where winter temperatures drop to −30 or −40 degrees Celsius. Snow leopards prey on wild ibex and Blue sheep in the most precipitous areas which are too dangerous for wolves. They prefer the eastern part of the country where they are found in open valleys and near villages – the kinds of place in which Snow leopards are never seen. Villagers have been defending themselves against the predation of wolves for hundreds of years. Many settlements are protected by traditional wolf-traps which are deep, stone-lined pits into which the wolf falls and from which it is unable to escape.

Wolves are regarded as pests in **Mongolia** where an official drive to exterminate both wolves and foxes has had far-reaching effects. Like wolves found in arid parts of the steppe in Russia, Asian wolves in Mongolia normally eat a substantial number of small mammals. Since the slaughter of canid predators, the fertile prairie that lies east of the Mongolian capital Ulan Batar – an area ten times as large as the Netherlands – has become overrun by a plague of rodents. As farmers struggle to protect their harvests they may come to re-evaluate the role of predators such as wolves and foxes.

Wild Bactrian camels (*Camelus bactrianus ferus*) only survive in and around the Great Gobi National Park in Mongolia and in neighbouring areas of western China. Their range is decreasing and their numbers are steadily falling because a drought that began in the early 1980s has caused many springs to dry up and the camel's principal food plant – a shrub called *Haloxylon ammondendron* – to die out. Lacking energy, the camels became particularly vulnerable to wolves, who are their main predators. So many young camels were being taken that the Park administration initiated a wolf-control programme in 1987 and now wolves are rarely seen in the Gobi National Park.

Wolf and fox-skins from Mongolia are regularly sold on the European market through the Leipzig fur auction, but in 1991 several hundred live pups were collected from dens around the country for sale to zoos in Europe. All of the same generation, these young wolves must have represented the entire year's progeny from a huge area. No one can say how many adults were killed in this sweep. It was instigated by a private entrepreneur who attempted to break international Convention on International Trade in Endangered Species (CITES) regulations by exporting the wolves to their final destinations via Hungary. Things went wrong. Hungarian officials are currently waging a war against contraband dealers and wildlife salesmen and the young wolves were instantly impounded. They should have been sent straight back to Mongolia in accordance with the CITES international agreement of the Washington Convention, but they were in such bad health – and it was certain that they would be shot on arrival – that Hungarian officials relented and permitted them to stay while attempts were made to find a new home. Things looked bleak for a while, but finally Brigitte Bardot and Friends of Animals came to the rescue. They took responsibility for the survivors and had them shipped to Gévaudan in southern France, where they are now the central attraction in a wolf park which lies on the wooded hillsides above the spectacular gorges of the Cévennes. The preserve is more than a zoo. It has been set up to reeducate the public about the real nature of wolves. During the eighteenth century the area of Gévaudan was ravaged by the attentions of a (probably rabid) wolf-pack which claimed the lives of over sixty people. The terrifying events of the period 1764–7 have never been entirely forgotten in France. However, now it's time to get events into perspective. Wild wolves are

In contries where populations of large prey, such as deer, have been exterminated by human overhunting, wolves must change their habits. They often hunt alone, killing small animals such as hares.

re-entering France across the Alps from Italy, establishing themselves in the Mercantour National Park, barely one hour from Nice. Although theoretically protected by law, they will need the sympathy of the French public if they are not to be shot.

Although wolves once occupied the whole of **China**, they have been eliminated from many provinces by the expansion of agriculture. The Chinese wolf, like its European counterpart, is cast in the role of villain in novels, poems and fairytales. Rabies is greatly feared in China where the worst-affected area – Heilongjiang in the north-east – still harbors wolves. Until recently pigs accounted for 46 per cent of the wolf's diet in this region, but livestock predation is no longer a problem because the wolf population has been savagely reduced, as it has over most of China, by a system of bounty hunting, den-digging and poisoning.

Wolves are still found in **Tibet (Xinjiang)** but even in remote areas their populations are in steep decline. The Taxkorgan Reserve lies on the borders of Pakistan, Tadzhikistan (formerly part of the USSR) and Afghanistan in the south-west corner of Xinjiang Uygur Autonomous Region. Although a Reserve,

Throughout the early summer months, hares and rabbits are carried back to the den in order to feed the pups.

this part of Tibet has been devastated by overgrazing and most of its trees have been cut for fuelwood. The situation is so desperate that even the shrubs are pulled up to burn their roots. Around 7,000 people inhabit the Reserve which also supports 70,000 domestic animals. Traditionally the Tajik and Kirgiz tribespeople supplement their diet with hunting, but an influx of outsiders – roadbuilders and military personnel – has resulted in serious overhunting. Ibex, Blue sheep and Marco Polo sheep are now hard to find, so the wolves occasionally prey on domestic sheep and yaks. The living standard of the tribespeople is very low and the loss of a single animal is a disaster. Even legally protected Snow leopards are killed if they are seen near the herds. Dr George Schaller, Science Director of Wildlife Conservation International (United States) has called for cooperation to set up one large international reserve to encompass the border regions of Afghanistan, Russia, Pakistan and China in order to safeguard the Snow leopard and to protect Marco Polo sheep which migrate from one country to another with the seasons. The Tibetan authorities are taking steps to protect their wildlife, but to be effective, they need assistance from their neighbors.

In 1990 the Environmental Protective Agency of the Chinese Republic announced that it intended to create a reserve in north-west Tibet – the Chang Tang Reserve – which would cover 100,000 square miles (160,000 sq km). This constitutes one-fifth of the country. With material help from Wildlife Conservation International they are not only establishing the largest natural reserve on earth, but are protecting one of the last pristine ecosystems known to man. It is reported that Chang Tang, in contrast to Taxkorgan, is an area of tremendous unspoilt natural beauty consisting of wide valleys, lakes and mountain ranges. Gazelle, antelope, wild sheep, wild ass, Brown bear and Snow leopard exist in natural densities, for this area is very sparsely inhabited by herdsmen. Wolves discovered here are of the subspecies *Canis lupus chanco* rather than the "woolly wolf" (*Canis lupus laniger*) found elsewhere in China.

Since 1992 the Tibetans have been defending the Chang Tang Reserve from the incursions of hunters searching for the Tibetan antelope (*Pantholops hodgsonii*). The wool from this antelope is known as *shahtoosh* (king of wool) and it is in demand by Nepalese and Kashmiri merchants who can sell a scarf made from this fiber for as much as 8,000 dollars. Eight antelopes must be killed to yield just 2 pounds (1 kg) of wool and demand is increasing from European manufacturers as well as Indian weavers.

The general decline of wolves throughout Eurasia is alarming but their conservation cannot be undertaken in isolation. Wolves need a healthy wild environment, rich in natural prey, if they are to live in peace with man. So many regions have been radically altered by agriculture that there is little wild habitat left for wolves to exploit. Preserving wolves in areas of high human habitation is inevitably a frustrating and expensive business. Conservation efforts, wherever they are undertaken around the world, are far better directed into preserving large areas of natural habitat for the benefit of all wildlife. Although very few Western people have been able to visit Chang Tang Reserve, its preservation may be seen in years to come as one of the most important contributions to world conservation in the twentieth century.

The endangered wolves of Asia, like this wolf from Mongolia, are likely to be best protected within the context of large international nature reserves set aside for the conservation of all wildlife.

141

CHAPTER TWELVE

RUN TO THE LAW...

We installed flashing highway lights at farms in response to thirty-six complaints, placed surveyor's flagging on farms in at least eight instances, and placed a combination strobe light-siren device at the problem site in six instances. These devices were used along with trapping in seventeen instances.

Steven H. Fritts, William J. Paul, L. David Mech, David P. Scott, Trends and Management of Wolf – Livestock conflicts in Minnesota (United States Department of the Interior, Fish and Wildlife Service Resource Publications, 181, Washington D.C., 1992)

The conservation of wolves is no easy matter. In areas that are shared by wolf and man, the predator needs permission to exist. In a few places, that permission has been granted in the form of legal protection, but only in the United States of America has that legal protection been seriously enforced. No other country has made such an effort to soften the interface between wolf and man. Nowhere else has there been such a bold attempt to harness the advances of modern technology to save the wolf, rather than kill it.

In Eurasian countries where wolves have always been regarded as vermin, their disappearance goes unremarked. Incomplete reports suggest that they are under tremendous human pressure over most of their range. Local races such as the Pale desert wolf from the Middle East, could disappear before anyone learns the details of their unique way of life. The twentieth century has probably seen the extinction of more species of plants and animals than at any other time during man's tenancy of the Earth. At last we are beginning to notice and to mourn the loss of natural diversity, but there is no time to waste.

The path to extinction is not very long. It need not be preceded by a steady decline in numbers. Extinction can occur almost overnight. The bison barely escaped. Not so the passenger pigeon which existed in such vast numbers during the nineteenth century that its extinction was unthinkable. The ornithologist Alexander Wilson calculated that a flock he observed in 1832 contained well over 2,000 million birds. Their flight was more than a mile wide and took four hours to pass him. Regarded universally as a pest, the passenger pigeons were indiscriminately shot. The last survivor – a hen called Martha – died in the Cincinnati Zoological Gardens on September 1, 1914. Because numbers are not a reliable guide to security, the name of the wolf is inscribed with over 5,000 others on the IUCN Red List of Threatened Species.

Some of the animals we think we have saved through our new interest in conservation – the bison, the Blue whale, the tiger, the Black rhino – may have only paused before saying goodbye. Turning back the tide of extinction is very hard, because once numbers get below a critical level the population becomes highly unstable and supervulnerable to disease, pollution and food shortages. One year the population will increase fantastically – only to plunge the following season. It is this instability, not overall numbers, which should sound the warning.

If we allow it, endangered subspecies of wolves can quickly recover. Unfortunately, the wolf issue still provokes tremendous fear. Perhaps the reason lies deep in the religious practices of our pagan prehistory. Perhaps the wolf's occasional role as carrier of rabies has given us cause to be nervous. Perhaps we like the excitement generated by the distant thrill of fear, purveyed quite safely by newspapers and television. All around the world, biologists are trying to counter subconscious antipathy to wolves by means of educational programs on the basis that if people understood a little more about these animals they would be likely to support conservation measures. Experience has shown that no recovery is possible without the cooperation of people who live in the area, the people whose property is at risk. But education takes time and time is running out. Legislation has caused a storm of protest in the United States, but the Endangered Species Act has made wolf recovery possible. Can the law bridge the gap between hatred and care in Europe?

There is no shortage of wild habitat suitable for wolves in **Scandinavia**, but wolf-mania is felt more passionately here than perhaps anywhere else in the world. For fifty years wolves were hardly seen in Norway and Sweden but during the 1980s they managed to breed several times, not above the Arctic Circle, but in southern Scandinavia where nobody expected them to turn up. The first to arrive in 1981 was an extraordinary animal. A solitary male, it regularly killed elk (moose) weighing up to 1,000 pounds (500 kg) unaided – a feat which normally taxes the resources of an entire pack. The following year a female joined him. She too was a wolf of tremendous skill and strength. Hunting together, they sometimes pulled down an elk apiece, caching the surplus meat under the snow. Their pups stirred up a storm of controversy in Sweden. Many were killed; run over by vehicles or illegally shot by hunters who founded a society for the destruction of the wolf. According to Swedish law, a shepherd may shoot a wolf that molests his flock but these wolf-killers were not shepherds and, time after time, they got away with it. When the alpha female herself was shot in 1985 by a man who owned no sheep, a prosecution was brought. The trial was marked by an angry demonstration staged by the anti-wolf brigade for the benefit of television cameras. Although the killer was not punished by the court, one of the cubs was found a few days later. It had been shot, then scalped and grotesquely mutilated. Hate-mail filled the post of the wolf-researchers who endeavoured to counter hysterical publicity in the press. In the years that followed wolves have quietly continued to breed in Sweden, but most have died. Some have been hounded – quite publicly – to their deaths. The total wolf population in Sweden and Norway is still only fourteen to sixteen wolves.

The Värmland Pack lives in a forest that straddles the border with Norway, an

Previous page: Wolves are extraordinary survivors. In Italy and Spain, where large wild prey are scarce, many have overcome their fear of man to scavenge from village rubbish dumps. However, the tips are gradually being closed down for public health reasons.

area boasting the highest density of elk (moose) in the world. Of course, the wolves sometimes wander over the international border. When they do, even the scanty protection they receive in Sweden is denied them. In Norway the only criterion required for shooting a wolf is the *belief* that it might kill stock!

Although the land of Odin has a particularly dark past as far as wolves are concerned, there may be some hope for the future. Norwegian conservationists are calling for complete protection in Hedmark, which would save the Värmland Pack. Meanwhile, in Sweden, a second wolf-pack is establishing itself in Jämtland, where a female gave birth to six cubs in 1991. An organization for the protection of the wolf has been set up by the local authority with the help of landowners, hunting societies and even a reindeer owner! However, in spite of their efforts to spread accurate information about wolves and to bring together the interests of farmers and preservationists, the local press continues to carry anti-wolf propaganda, and the new pack has received a typically mixed welcome.

Scandinavian wolves are finding recovery difficult although a large and healthy population exists in nearby Karelia, an independent state within the Russian Federation. Lying on the eastern border of Finland, this area was ceded by the Finns to the Russians as part of a package of war reparations. After the war, conditions in Karelia became distinctly favorable towards wolves which, until that time, had not existed there in large numbers. Farmland was left to run wild and Soviet foresters clear-felled large areas of coniferous forest, replanting with deciduous trees. This change in habitat led to an increase in elk (moose) numbers and a consequent rise in the wolf population, which trebled in less than a decade to reach what is probably its natural saturation point – an estimated 900 wolves in 1976. Over the border, alarmed Finnish reindeer herders mounted the most efficient wolf-killing program in the world, making daily patrols across the snow to track down immigrants from Karelia. As a result of their vigilance, Finland has a very low wolf population – less than 100 – and few wolves from Karelia succeed in crossing Finnish territory alive to reach Norway or Sweden.

The virtual extirpation of wolves from Scandinavia was possible because the population was effectively cut off from contact with other wolves in Europe. Anywhere that wolf "lifelines" are broken, wolves are in danger. If hunting does not wipe them out, inbreeding or cross-breeding with dogs will finish them off. The fragile recovery in Norway and Sweden needs new blood if it is to stand a chance of survival. The area devoted to reindeer husbandry in northern Finland makes up almost half the country and in this area wolves are not tolerated. However, further south wolves cause very little damage amongst livestock (there are no reindeer) and protection for wolves is possible. Finland has signed the Bern Convention, undertaking to protect nature but it continues to make an exception of the wolf.

The Bern Convention of the Council of Europe is the only serious piece of international legislation to attempt to protect wildlife in Europe. The wolf is listed in Appendix II of the 1979 Convention on the Conservation of European Wildlife and Natural Habitats (Bern). It is designated a "strictly protected fauna species" and is entitled to be "specially protected." Every country that signs the Convention has agreed to prohibit the killing and capture of wolves, to prohibit damage or destruction of breeding and resting sites, to prohibit deliberate disturbance and especially to prevent the trade in wolves and their skins. The

Spanish Mastine dogs are bred and trained to protect domestic animals from wolves. Horses are particularly vulnerable to attack, especially when they are left hobbled and unable to defend themselves, like this one.

wolf is also listed in Appendix II of the 1973 Convention on International Trade in Endangered Species of Wild Fauna and Flora (CITES) which bans the trade of endangered animals.

Under current international legislation, the wolf is (in theory) protected by law in Norway and Sweden, as it is in Portugal and Italy too, but prosecutions are rare and punishment almost unheard of. The Bern Convention does not work because it is not enforceable. Its legislation is impossible to implement because it permits member states to take out derogations to exclude the wolf, which enable them to carry on campaigns of extermination as before. Although the biological investigative work of the Committee of the Council of Europe has led to the issuing of clear directives designed to protect Europe's shrinking wolf populations, the Convention can enforce nothing. In 1989, wolf experts meeting under the auspices of the Standing Committee of the Bern Convention,

recommended that the countries of Fennoscandia should draw up a joint management plan. In 1993 nothing has yet been announced. In the United States the much maligned but very effective Endangered Species Act (see Chapter 8) works because it is enforced on a federal basis. Political differences at state level cannot alter it.

The Bern Convention is particularly difficult to uphold in **Spain** where the wolf is classed as a game animal. This category does allow some degree of protection, but as local administrations handle nature conservation on an individual basis, there is considerable variation in the way it is exercised. Wolves are officially shot in National Parks, while the owners of private hunting estates seem to manage wildlife as they see fit. While Andalucia completely protects its small wolf population and pays compensation for wolf predation, in Galicia the wolf is still hunted and poisoned. In spite of the killing, wolves have been making a recovery in Spain and the population has risen to over 1,500. Nevertheless, wolves remain vulnerable because they are often isolated from each other and cut off from other populations in Europe. Most of them are found in the inaccessible mountainous parts of Galicia and in Asturias and Leon. Lower densities of wolves exist along the Spanish–Portuguese border, mainly in Estremadura. Dispersing wolves from this area sometimes wander into Portugal. An isolated population exists in the Sierra Morena in northern Andalusia and a few wolves are now establishing themselves in the Alava–Longrono area of north-east Spain.

Slowly returning after an absence of nearly one hundred years, a small number of wolves are reestablishing themselves in Sweden. Public opinion has been running against them, although Scandinavia has large herds of European elk (American moose) and extensive areas of wilderness where wolf packs could exist in peace. Norway, Sweden and Finland are signatories to the Bern Convention, but little action is taken against hunters who kill wolves illegally.

Resistance to the idea of conservation has been vigorous from hunters and farmers, although an intensive public education campaign has changed the attitudes of most Spaniards from fear to concern and interest in the species. But old ways die hard. When wolves made a reappearance in the Carrnaza Valley in Biscaia in the Basque country – an area devoted to cattle-rearing – farmers held a *batida*, then strung up the bodies of the dead wolves in public.

The annual damage to livestock was estimated at nearly 1 million dollars in 1987, a figure disproportionately high in the mountain area of Cantabria where livestock are left to range freely. Sheep, goats and horses are the usual victims and as the local Junta seldom pays any compensation to farmers, the wolf is detested. Research by the National Conservation Branch of the Ministry of Agriculture (ICONA) has shown that damage to livestock is far more closely related to poor agriculture practices than to wolf density. The lowest rate of damage in Spain occurs where wolves are most numerous, partly because of the existence of natural prey, but also because livestock is better cared for.

While the hunting lobby is extremely powerful, farmers in northern Spain could be described as a law unto themselves. During the first six weeks of 1989 the country was set ablaze by shepherds intent on increasing their pasturage. At least 530 fires caused the destruction of 167 square miles (43,152 hectares) of meadow scrub and woodland. Robbed of their natural habitat displaced wolves were seen in the open, which led people to believe that the countryside was "overrun" and to demand that the wolves should be killed.

Conflict with wolves is frequent because the human population in rural Galicia is dense; more than fifty people per square kilometer (0.386 mile). Feeling runs high because wolves feed mainly on livestock and on village refuse dumps. However, this is not the case in other areas of Spain. Further south, in Estremadura and Sierra Morena, wolves occupy undisturbed, almost uninhabited areas of natural habitat where they feed on red deer.

Another signatory to the Bern Convention is **Portugal**. Here the wolf population is estimated to be about 200, mostly found in the north. A group of conservationists called Grupo Lobo has long been campaigning for stricter hunting laws and a ban on traps, poisons and the trade in skins. In 1988 their views were supported when a new law was introduced conferring complete legal protection on the wolf. Compensation is the cornerstone to the new legislation, for it is promised that farmers who lose stock will be reimbursed. Unfortunately, the Park Service which is responsible under the new legislation for making payments to farmers was not granted a budget to do so! By January 1993 shepherds had understandably lost patience with government and conservationists alike. They formed The Shepherds' League, a society dedicated to exterminate the wolf.

Grupo Lobo is one of the most influential ginger-groups in Europe to fight on behalf of the wolf. As well as running an educational centre which introduces captive wolves to the public, it is pressing for the improvement of wolf habitats and the protection of deer. Uncontrolled hunting is still rife, even inside National Parks. The editor of the Grupo Lobo *Newsletter* (February 1, 1991) writes; "Ironically, the only areas where hunting is (ever) prohibited are hunting reserves!" There are more than 400,000 licensed hunters in Portugal as well as many thousands of poachers. An astonishing 34 percent of the population

describe themselves as hunters and their continual disturbance has not only reduced populations of deer to critical levels but is preventing mammals and birds from breeding within designated nature reserves. Thanks to hunters almost all the known nesting sites of the Golden eagle have been deserted in the National Park of Peneda-Gerês.

There are so few wild deer in **Italy** that wolves must scavenge on rubbish tips or kill sheep and goats to survive. It is not shepherds who are the greatest threat to wolves. The inhabitants of the mountains have lived alongside wolves for thousands of years and regard them with equanimity. The real threat comes once again from Italy's 2 million hunters who seldom refrain from shooting wolves if they encounter a pack while chasing fox or wild boar. Although wolves are protected on paper, 70 percent of them die through "mistaken identity".

Only 250 wolves survive in Italy, mostly found in the central and southern Apennines. They are divided into ten distinct groups, each separated from the others by deep valleys which hold a substantial human population. The wolves are often seen around the villages and there is a continuous exchange of wolves between the various areas. At altitudes of 2,400–4,500 feet (800–1,500 m), the mountains are covered by beech forest interspersed with pasture which is devoted to cattle and sheep. Wolves are also found in typical Mediterranean shrubby habitat just 30 miles (50 km) north of Rome as well as in southern Tuscany.

Italian wolves lead very different lives to those of their American cousins for

Lone wolves, like those who started the recolonization of Norway and Sweden, risked everything when they left the security of their birth pack in Karelia to search for a mate. Scent marks along the trail, together with howling, enabled the first pioneers to find each other.

Dogs are normally afraid to approach wolves for fear of being eaten, but where the wolf population is very low, mating between dogs and wolves can occur. This results in hybrids which may be physically indistinguishable from wild wolves.

The Rio Cares, Covadonga, acts as a refuge for Spanish wolves. Research has shown that losses of domestic livestock to wolves are highest where animals are left on the mountains unsupervised. Where agricultural practices are good, wolves cause little trouble.

there are no large wilderness areas left. The human population density is approximately 185 per square kilometer which means wolves live very close to their two greatest enemies. Italians claim to love animals and almost everyone owns a dog. However, pet ownership does not necessarily imply responsibility. A survey has shown that there are at least 3.5 million dogs in Italy. Some 600,000 of them are considered to be free-ranging, 200,000 are strays, and 80,000 are classed as feral. The traditional open garbage tip, thickly strewn with household rubbish and enriched daily by offal from the local slaughterhouse, provides a convenient meeting place. Generally dogs stay away from wolves, who sometimes kill and eat them, but when a bitch comes into heat, a lonely male wolf may cover her. The result is a hybrid.

If the pups turn out to resemble their mother, they have a passport to enter villages and farms at any time of day or night, for nobody will look twice at them. In fact, feral dogs and hybrids – like wolves – are generally nocturnal and shy of man. Research has shown that most of the damage to livestock perpetrated by dogs is the work of the free-ranging category, those who go home at the end of the day.

As wolf-hybrids become more common, true wolves are threatened by genetic contamination. It is ironic that the wolf could be extirpated, not by gunfire, poison or traps but by another animal, a creature so similar to itself that some scientists have claimed they are the same species. Dogs lack the intricate social structure of wolves. Without the domination of an alpha pair, there is no birth

Yes, He Killed Cattle, to Eat
But Did He Deserve This?

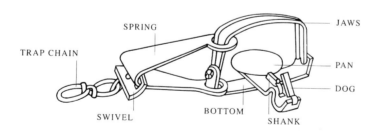

The leg-hold or gin trap is still the most common method of trapping wild animals for the fur trade. The wolf steps on the pan which acts as a trigger to release powerful steel jaws, catching the animal alive. Perhaps the worst aspect of the leg-hold trap is the length of time that the animal is held in agony before the trapper returns to kill it. Fifteen hours is said to be the average, but some trappers check their traplines only once every few days. Wolves make frantic efforts to escape, sometimes getting away by gnawing off their own foot. Many non-target animals, such as eagles, owls and domestic pets can be snared, for the leg-hold trap does not discriminate.

control, and with feral dogs breeding twice a year, the dog problem is bound to get worse over the next few years. Animal protection societies will not allow the dogs to be slaughtered, even though their existence could spell extinction for the Italian wolf. The law, it seems, is powerless to help. In a last-ditch attempt to save a few pure wolves, biologists have started a captive-breeding program, but until the dogs are gone, release is probably a waste of time.

Perhaps the fur trade makes a mockery of the law more cynically than any other vested interest. On November 4, 1991 the Council of the European Community adopted Resolution Number 3254/91. It was a bold resolution designed to worry the furriers of London and Frankfurt. It prohibited the import into the Community of pelts and manufactured goods made from beaver, otter, coyote, wolf, lynx, bobcat, racoon, muskrat, fisher, badger and ermine, to take effect from January 1, 1995, "unless the trapping methods used meet internationally recognized standards" and "unless sufficient progress is being made in developing humane methods of trapping."

You can imagine the trappers' reactions. "Is this some kind of joke? The EC wants a 'nice' way to kill wild animals?"

No. Resolution Number 3254/91 is a piece of necessary legislation that has arrived on the international agenda not a moment too soon. Leg-hold traps are the standard way of catching wolves as well as many other creatures for the fur trade. The trap doesn't damage the pelt, it just holds the animal in indescribable agony until the hunter gets around to checking his trapline. That could be five days or more.

Around 4 million animals are trapped this way in Canada, 21 million in the United States, and 15 million in Canada and the former USSR. Although it is illegal, a leg-hold trap designed to catch wolves is manufactured and sold in Portugal.

Would any sensitive person wear skins they knew were acquired this way? Of course not! So the fur trade vigorously resisted the idea of labeling coats made out of pelts caught in leg-hold traps. Then, to get around that inconvenient EC Resolution, they negotiated with the International Standards Organization (ISO). This body thought it would be easier to redefine the word "humane" than address the problem of cruelty. Leg-hold traps that break legs or dislocate joints, together with "submersion" traps that take ten minutes to drown a muskrat are fine . . . just fine in their opinion. From henceforth they are to be described as "humane" and pelts derived from them will continue to be imported into the EC. They will probably be labeled too . . . "humane."

So what is the law worth? In spite of the obvious shortcomings of legislation, I believe it is an invaluable aid to changing attitudes. On its own it can achieve little. Nothing can replace the lengthy process of education, the seemingly endless round of visiting schools, attending public meetings, showing films and writing pamphlets to win hearts and minds. At the same time little can be achieved without that special moral quality that being on the right side of the law confers.

The problem with protecting wolves in Eurasia lies in the fact that in many countries there may be a genuine need for control. In agricultural areas where there is a shortage of natural prey, the presence of wolves brings financial hardship. Each wild wolf costs the Spanish authorities an average of 500 dollars a year in compensation, which is the equivalent in value to six sheep or one calf.

An 'omega' wolf shows its teeth in a grimace of active submission.

Opposite: A European wolf pack rests contentedly. In 1993, the Government of Brandenburg announced the presence of four wolves, together with the news that a female wolf had given birth. The survival of these wolves is precarious, and will depend on reeducating the public to abandon old fears and hatred.

In Italy the figure is substantially higher. In some circumstances controlling wolf numbers through culling may be the wisest course, but there are other options. The use of radio-collars to monitor the movements of wild wolves has shown that where wild prey is available, most wolves ignore domestic stock. Wolves can be trapped and relocated; they can be dissuaded from approaching farms. Death is not the only way.

The law is an imperfect tool but at the moment it is all we have to stop the runaway forces of commercial self-interest that will otherwise destroy our common future. The law forces everyone to consider alternatives. The next two years will see a titanic battle of wills displayed in the United States as the renewal of the Endangered Species Act is debated in Congress. Industry, farmers and local governments will argue that its restrictions block development. Preservationists will demand its extension to save even more species. An alternative to highlighting the protection of rare species such as the wolf and the

Spotted owl – a strategy that, as discussed in Chapter 8, has caused tremendous public antagonism – may be to hammer out legislation that protects entire ecosystems before they are irreparably damaged. I suspect that cast-iron protection for a basic list of vulnerable species will always be needed. Predators like wolves need special protection so that the intention of the legislature is crystal-clear.

The Bella Coola Indians of North America say that a shaman once tried to change all the animals in the world into men, but his magic only succeeded in transforming the eyes of the wolf. According to the Indians, wolves are "the only other human thing in the world."

To engage the eye of the wolf is to participate in what the writer Barry Lopez in his book *Of Wolves and Men* calls "the conversation of death". No human can adequately describe the bone-chilling effect of the predator's stare. Only the wolf's prey, in what is likely to be the last moment of its life on earth, can fully experience the amber intensity of that gaze; a mixture of ferocity, caution and calculation. If it is courageous, the prey will answer back with a penetrating stare of its own, a sign of its determination to sell its life as dearly as possible. Those who have watched this interaction say that, for a crucial moment, there is a battle of wills as predator and prey appear to decide together what shall happen next. Sometimes nothing happens; the wolf lopes off, the deer rejoins its herd. Sometimes there is a kill.

This conversation of death is not unique to canids. All predators that take risks must learn to weigh the consequences of their actions. The situation of the human race is particularly fascinating, for here is an animal that has also evolved a social organization and entertains relationships which are so similar to those of wolves that the words used to describe them – love, jealousy, rivalry, fear – can be applied to both species. We are fascinated by wolves because we understand them. We know the excitement of risk.

Like wolves, we love and protect those nearest to us, but we compete ruthlessly with those we regard as strangers. Our social organization into families, clans related by brotherhood, nations and, ultimately, federations, is an attempt to put aside aggression and to exploit the environment in a way that is sustainable. To agree a strategy that works for all of us.

However, agreement is hard to achieve. War and its attendant destruction are endemic in the human race. Even within our own communities we seem to be holding a "conversation of death" as we engage the vision of corporations and individual profiteers who sincerely believe that they have the right to short-term prosperity at the expense of the natural environment on which all life depends. They are slow to understand that conservation is not a luxury. Populations trends are such that the alternatives to caring for the environment are horrifying.

The wolf has already become a "flagship" species in North America, for it is an animal whose conservation is seen as a crucial part of our commitment towards nature. It is time for European and Asian countries to join together in planning a future for the wolf within significant areas of natural habitat that must be designated as international reserves.

It is time to set aside old fears. The wolf has always been an emblem of life and death in one. It is an important species, not because it is rare, but because it demands that we reassess our own impact on nature.

The dark wolf of the imagination was created in an age in which the threat of rabies combined with fear of the occult.

BIBLIOGRAPHY

Bibikov, D. I., *The Wolf,* Nauka, Moscow (in Russian), 1985

Blanco, J. C., Cuesta, L. and Reig, S., *El Lobo* (Canis lupus) *Situacion, Problematica y Apuntes Sobre Su Ecologica,* (in Spanish) Ministerio de Agricultura Pesca y Alimentacion, 1990

Burton, Robert, *Carnivores of Europe,* Batsford, 1979

Douglas, A., *The Beast Within: A History of the Werewolf,* Chapmans Publishers Ltd., 1992

Fiennes, Richard, *The Order of Wolves,* Hamish Hamilton Ltd., 1976

Fox, M. W., *Behaviour of Wolves, Dogs and Related Canids,* Jonathan Cape, 1971

Fox, M. W., *The Wild Canids,* Van Nostrand Reinhold Company, 1975

Fritts, S. H., William, J. P., Mech, L. David and Scott, David P., *Trends and Management of Wolf-Livestock Conflicts In Minnesota,* US Fish And Wildlife Service, Resource Publication 181, 1992

Graves, Robert, *Greek Myths,* Cassell Ltd., 1955

Harrison, D. L. and Bates, P. J. J., *The Mammals of Arabia,* Harrison Zoological Museum Publication, 1991

Hinde, Thomas, *Forests of Britain,* Victor Gollancz Ltd., 1985

Jhala, Y. V. and Giles Jr, R. H., 'The Status and Conservation of the Wolf in Gujarat and Rajasthan, India', *Conservation Biology,* Vol. 5, No. 4, December, 1991

Knystautas, Algirdas, *The Natural History of the USSR,* Century, 1987

Komarov, Boris, *The Destruction of Wildlife in the Soviet Union,* M. E. Sharpe Inc. NY, 1980

Leslie Jnr, D. M. and Tissescu, Alexandru, 'Beyond The Danube Delta: Forest Conservation and Research Opportunities in Romania', *Conservation Biology,* Vol. 6, No. 2, June, 1992

Macdonald, D., *The Velvet Claw,* BBC Books, 1992

MacLysaght, Edward, *Irish Life in the Seventeenth Century* (3rd Edn.), Cork, 1969

Malson, Lucien and Itard, Jean, *Wolf Children and the Wild Boy of Aveyron,* Union Generale d'Editions (Trans. NLB London 1972), 1964

Mech, L. David, *The Wolf,* The Natural History Press, 1970

Mech, L. David, *The Way of the Wolf,* Swan Hill Press, 1991

Murie, A., *The Wolves of Mount McKinley,* Fauna Of The National Parks Of The United States, Fauna Series 5 US Government Printing Office, Washington, 1944

Ognev, S. I., *Mammals of Eastern Europe and Northern Asia,* Vol. 2, Carnivora, Fissipedia, 1932 (Israel Program for Scientific Translation), 1962

Pendlesonn, K. R. G., *The Vikings,* Windward, 1980

Polish Academy Of Sciences, *Atlas of Polish Mammals,* PWN Panstwowe Wydawnictwo Naukowe, 1983

Pulliainen, E., 'Studies of the Wolf in Finland', *Ann. Zool. Fenn. 2,* 1965

Pulliainen, E. and Dummer-Stolte, K., *Wolves in Finland,* International Wolf, 1992

Rackham, Oliver, *The History of the Countryside,* Dent, 1986

Schaller, G. B., Li Hong, Lu Hua, Ren Junrang, Qiu Mingjiang and Wang Haibin, 'Status of Large Mammals in the Taxkorgan Reserve, Xinjiang, China', *Biological Conservation,* Vol. 42, 1987

Sparks, B. W. and West, R. G., *The Ice Age in Britain,* Methuen Library (reprint), 1981

Summers, M., *The Werewolf,* Kegan Paul, 1933

Thomas, Keith, *Man and the Natural World,* Allen Lane, 1983

Wimberly, L. C., *Folklore in the English and Scottish Ballads,* University of Chicago Press, 1928

Zimen, Erik, *The Wolf,* Souvenir Press, 1981

INDEX

PICTURE ACKNOWLEDGEMENTS

American Heritage Center, University of Wyoming, USA 152; Antikvarisk-topografiska arkivet, Stockholm 28; Arizona Historical Society, Helena 95, 105; Joel Bennett 126, 137, 140; Bomford/Borkowski 128, 130; J. Bradshaw 16, 34, 38, 46, 74, 114, 122; c The British Library 27, 47; c The British Museum 26; The Board of Trinity College, Dublin 43; Steven Fritts 98, 99; Giellie/Odyssey/Impact 117; John Harris/Survival Anglia 91; Hulton Deutsch Collection Limited 36, 37, 42, 44, 45, 156; Erik Isakson 147; Italian Tourist Board 29; Paul Johnson/Survival Anglia 113; R. Kemp vi-v, 6, 10, 12, 15, 20(bottom), 61, 65, 70, 77, 79, 80, 83, 87(both), 90, 92, 100, 102, 108, 110, 111, 112, 118, 119; R & J Kemp 55, 62, 64, 66, 67, 68, 75, 82, 106, 107, 133, 138, 139, 142, 146, 149, 150, 151, 154; R Kemp/G Hatherley 88; R & J Kemp/Survival Anglia 54, 57, 58, 59(both), 155; Mansell Collection 33, 39, 41; Mary Evans Picture Library 21, 32, 40; L David Mech 53, 60, 78; Montana Historical Society 94; The National Museum, Copenhagen 22; Piermont Morgan Library, New York. M 736, f. 16v. 25; Heather Quinn 18, 152 (illustrations); Ruth Rulland/Simon Paneak Memorial Museum 20 (top); L. Ryabov 123, 124; A Shoob, Department of Zoology, Tel Aviv University 9(all), 134, 135; Maurice and Carroll Tibbles 50; Walters Art Gallery, Baltimore 24; Konrad Wothe/Survival Anglia ii. End paper maps by Raymond Turvey.

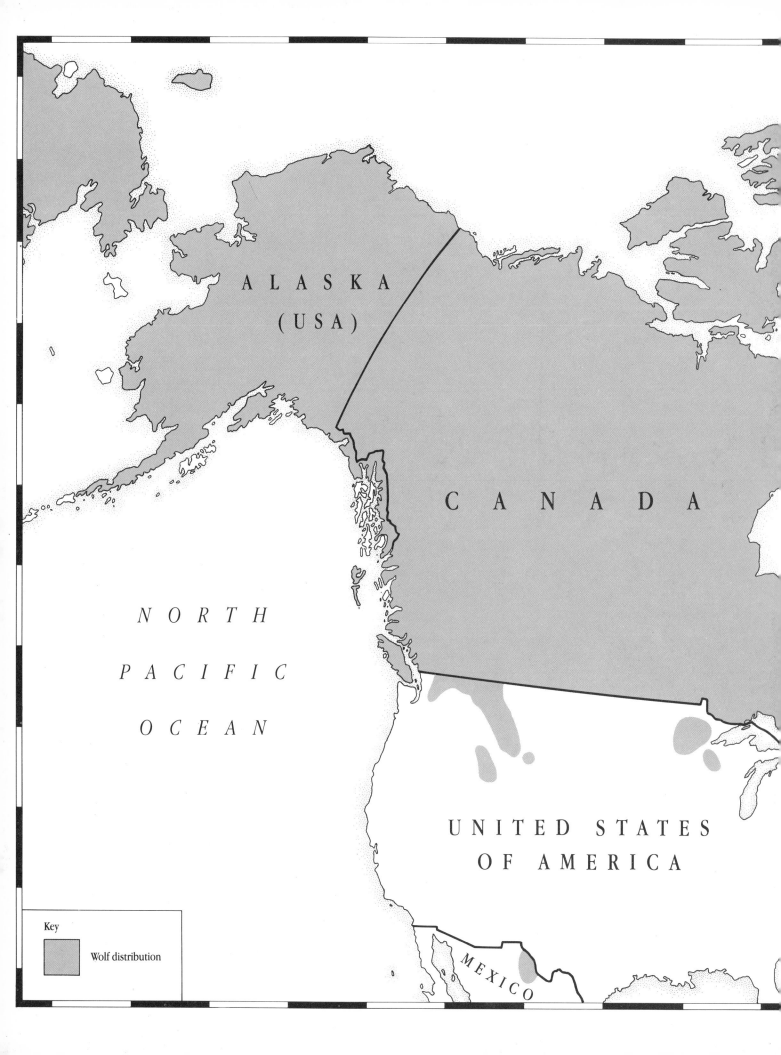

ALASKA
(USA)

CANADA

NORTH

PACIFIC

OCEAN

UNITED STATES
OF AMERICA

MEXICO

Key

Wolf distribution